Getting the Most from
Literature
Groups

by
Penny Strube

SCHOLASTIC
PROFESSIONAL BOOKS

NEW YORK • TORONTO • LONDON • AUCKLAND • SYDNEY

Dedication

I want to dedicate this book to God for giving me the Living Word, to my husband, Lynn, without whom I would never have met the literary character of Dirk Pitt, to my daughter, Carrianne, for teaching me a teenager's interpretation of *Great Expectations*, and to my son, Levi, for teaching me how much fun nonfiction books can be.

Cover design by Vincent Ceci and Jaime Lucero
Book design and diagrams by Carmen Robert Sorvillo
Copyright © 1996 by Penny Strube
Printed in USA

12 11 10 9 8 7 6 5 4   8 7/9

Table of Contents

Chapter 1
Why I Teach with Literature 4

Chapter 2
Selecting and Collecting Good Books 15

Chapter 3
When Children Choose Literature 23

Chapter 4
First Group Session 33

Chapter 5
Independent Reading 42

Chapter 6
Using Literature Response Logs 48

Chapter 7
Literature Study Groups in Action 58

Chapter 8
Literature Extensions and Responses 65

Chapter 9
Strategies for Further Interaction with Text 76

Chapter 10
Assessment and Evaluation 88

Appendix
Blank Reproducible Forms 105

Chapter 1

Why I Teach with Literature

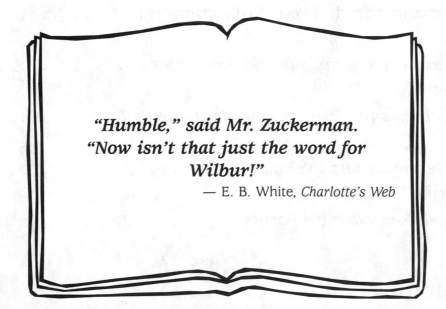

*"Humble," said Mr. Zuckerman.
"Now isn't that just the word for
Wilbur!"*

— E. B. White, *Charlotte's Web*

My "Humble" Beginnings

When I reflect on my reading background, it seems to me that Wilbur and I have much in common: I too had a very humble beginning. I grew up with Dick and Jane, went to college when basal instruction was the focus, and signed a contract in a traditional school district. All this contributed to my unfamiliarity with the use of real literature in my classroom. Teaching reading to my students was simply an extension of the way in which I had learned to read. I felt good about this method, because I was giving the children the same experiences I had been given. However, I never stopped to reflect upon myself as a reader.

In the elementary grades, I'd read only pre-chosen reading material. Worksheets were completed and colored without much thought as to the purpose of the activity. My middle and high school years consisted of required reading in all subjects. A list of required reading was my only reason for picking up a book. During the undergraduate college years, I read for survival. Each class had required assignments for course completion. Reading for pleasure was not something I remember from my childhood, adolescence, or young adult years. But when I decided to return to graduate school for a higher degree, my attitude toward reading changed.

Sunny — An Aptly Named Teacher

I met Sunny in graduate school. She was not like any other professor that I had ever had! Sunny demonstrated what was to me a unique approach to teaching reading. Each time we met for class, Sunny would literally drag in a bag of books that she would read aloud. She raised the books high and read to us just as though we were small children. At the time I didn't make the connection, but I *was* just a child when it came to knowing what reading was all about. Sunny encouraged the whole graduate class to take the books home and enjoy re-reading them. She dropped the names of authors as if she knew them personally. Sunny introduced our class to what we later referred to as "bookstore hopping." We'd pile into several cars, drive to many bookstores located throughout the St. Louis area, and spend hours poring over children's books. Sunny awakened me to the possibility that there was something missing in my reading program.

I was teaching fourth grade at the time. For children of that age, the basal reader offered only excerpts of "real" books— usually one or two chapters of a book to read, study, and dissect. It never occurred to me that there was more for students in *Charlotte's Web* than just those one or two rich chapters. Sunny had whetted my appetite, so that I was eager to present that "more" to my students; but I knew that I first had to learn more about literature.

Dorothy — My Mentor

At about this time, our school district invited a professor from the University of Missouri to speak to us about literature. I had neither heard of nor met Dr. Dorothy Watson. I entered the appointed workshop classroom to find all the chalk rails lined with children's books. Out of the fifty or so that she had on display, I'm ashamed to say that I was familiar with only a few. They were the award-winners that I'd read and written book reviews on during an undergraduate children's literature class. Dr. Watson's approach to books was totally unexpected. From the chalk rails, she picked up one book at a time. She didn't talk about the book.

She told about the conversations that children had had with each other as they read the books. Conversations! Dorothy did not ask questions that required a correct answer. She simply related the conversations of children. The children's conversations were so full of meaning and insight. (They were nothing like the discussions that took place in my reading classes!) Her anecdotes totally mesmerized me. I left the workshop with a new energy toward teaching reading. My enthusiasm led me to read books written by researchers in the field of literature, to search out educational publications on literature, and to enroll in graduate classes in teaching literature.

❧

Authentic Books

Sunny and Dorothy had opened my eyes to the benefits of teaching with authentic books. By "authentic books" I mean the kinds of books that children encounter wherever their journeys take them. Authentic books contain a whole story (beginning, middle, end) written by an author with a purpose and a theme. According to Ralph Peterson and Maryann Eeds in *Grand Conversations* (Scholastic, 1990), the foundation for learning and teaching with literature is built on four beliefs:

- Story is a way to explore and enrich life.
- Interpretation comes from readers actively engaged in the reading process of making meaning by what they bring to and take from the text.
- Children have the innate ablity of being meaning makers.
- Dialogue provides the best means of understanding and explaining literature.

A literature-based approach has several distinguishing differences from a basal approach. The literature-based approach stems from a reading perspective that reflects a philosophy of how children learn to read.

In a literature-based classroom:
- Children choose their own books.
- Children choose books that fit their own purposes.
- Children use strategies to sample the text.
- Children interpret what they read.
- Children respond to the text verbally and in written form (see box below).

A Word on Children's Responses to Text

The initial response to the literature is a written reflection. The students engage in silent reading of the text, and then they record their reactions to the text by writing in a literature log or journal. The written response reveals immediate and personal reaction to the text.

After the individual written response to the chosen story, the literature group members meet somewhere in the classroom to discuss their individual responses to the literature. They talk one at a time and share personal reactions to the characters and events of the story. By sharing verbally, the children reveal to one another their thoughts and concerns about the ideas the literature created in their minds.

So What Is Reading?

At the beginning of the school year, I always ask my students what they think reading is. This is a sample of some frequent responses:
— "It is when you look at a word and understand it."
— "To get to know things."
— "Reading is something that's fun and educational."
— "Reading is an adventure."
— "Reading is a bunch of letters put together with spaces in between words."
— "I think reading is learning."
— "It is about someone or something and like a little world."
— "Reading is spelling."
— "Learning how to do stuff like math, directions, and driving."
— "I think reading is something you have to use your whole life."
— "Reading is what you are doing right now. You read what others write."
— "Reading is fun!"

Reading Is a Meaning-Making Process

I am not sure when I first realized that reading is a process. It might have been when, under the leadership of Carol Gilles, another professor at the University of Missouri, I took an in-depth look at reading along with many of my colleagues. We all agreed that reading was not just the ability to recognize a written word, or even knowing the meaning of that word in isolation. Reading is the connection made between the reader and the written words of the text. This connection implies more than just a simple

understanding. It is a comprehension that includes the reader's environment, past experiences, prior knowledge, and interpretation of language. The connection between the reader and the text suggests a simple interaction, but in reality, it is complex; in part because each reader brings a rich set of elements to the connection.

Because each child has had unique experiences, comes from a different environment, and owns individual prior knowledge, each reader has distinctively personal interpretations of language. That's what makes the reader-text connection more than just the simple interaction it seems at first.

Helping Readers Make Meaning: Language Cueing Systems

And as the reader interprets the text, bringing her own meaning and understanding to bear, she is assisted by the use of three 'cueing systems' that are part of the reading process. The systems are the **graphophonic,** the **syntactic,** and the **semantic.** To understand what is happening when children read, it is important to understand the cueing systems and their functions.

The **graphophonic** cueing system deals with the sound/symbol relationship, which includes the spelling of words and the sounds that the letters and letter combinations make. Punctuation is also a valuable part of this cueing system. Readers use this system to see if a word looks and sounds correct. The **syntactic** cueing system concentrates on how words, sentences, and paragraphs work together to structure the language. This system is associated with grammar. The third system, the **semantic** cueing system, pertains to the reader's environment and individual experiences. This cueing system brings a richness to the Literature Study Group, because the reader uses it to make sense of the context (Goodman, Watson, and Burke. *Reading Miscue Inventory*, Richard C. Owen, 1987). The reader uses all three cueing systems to comprehend, or arrive at, meaning from written language.

❦

How Authentic Literature Helps Students Make Meaning

Frank Smith, a pioneer in educational research, demonstrated that children learn to read by reading (*Reading Without Nonsense*, Teacher's College Press, 1985). When children are in a text-rich environment where they read and write for a real purpose, they will learn to construct meaning from the text. The teacher encourages and leads the children to become meaning-makers. The teacher facilitates the learning by interacting with the students to bring about a greater comprehension of the literature.

Using literature helps children see themselves as readers who create meaning. Children believe they are readers when:
1. Their own thoughts create meaning from the text.
2. They tell others what they believe the text means.

3. They become good listeners to other interpretations.
(Peterson, R., and Eeds, M. *Grand Conversations*, Scholastic, 1990)

❦

How Literature Groups Help Readers Make Meaning

Comprehension comes through the reader's link between his or her own experiences and the text. It is easy to comprehend the written word when you have had a personal experience similar in nature to the one being described. If you haven't, you can only imagine what the text is trying to convey. As I began to think about how often I had asked my students, "How many of you have been to a zoo, a museum, a ball game, etc.," only to have them answer "none," I realized then why they often didn't understand simple ideas in the stories they were reading. From first-graders not knowing that a polar bear was white, to fourth-graders having no idea what a vendor at a baseball game was doing throwing peanuts to the fans, I realized that the reader's experiences were critical to comprehension.

The reader's prior knowledge also plays a large role in comprehending the text. Often, in my attempt to stretch my own knowledge, I have decided to read a book that I might label "Heavy Reading," only to find that much of the language is meaningless to me. Because of my limited knowledge of the subject, or lack of related vocabulary, I've been at a loss to make much meaning of the text. This is essentially what happens to children on a regular basis. Since their prior knowledge is limited, children have a harder time grasping the meaning of the text.

The question is: Where do you gather background experiences or prior knowledge, when you are a child and your environment confines you to a limited existence? The answer that works for me is a heterogeneously grouped Literature Study Group.

Creating a Community of Readers

When students work together, they collaborate. When they work alone, they compete. In a Literature Study Group, there is no reason for competition. The goal is to discuss the meaning of the text in terms of possibilities, not in terms of exact answers for specific questions. Collaboration opens up a world of possibilities to the whole group. According to Ralph Peterson, there is a big advantage in having children with diverse interests, backgrounds, and experiences work together. They learn to work and exist together (*Life in a Crowded Place*, Heinemann, 1992). Building a community of learners creates an environment conducive to making meaning. When a community of readers shares interpretations, they create different interpretations that intensify the meaning-making possibilities for the whole group. Children who practice with experienced meaning makers learn to create meaning on their own (Peterson, Eeds, 1990).

Collaboration within the community of readers enhances learning through others' experiences, but *trust* must be the central focus of the group. Since many children come to school with limited life experiences, having children share experiences enriches the learning of all. Literature study groups give readers the opportunity to express their experiences in a relaxed, non-threatening atmosphere. Sharing personal experiences creates a sense of trust, confidence, and involvement with the other students in the group. Trust is the key that enables the community of learners to share ideas without reservation. Students begin to value the time they share with the group members and look forward to creating new ideas with the group.

In the beginning of the year, I use a mini-lesson to introduce Literature Study Groups to my students.

Defining Literature Groups

A literature group (or Literature Study Group or circle) is a group of readers who have in common the fact that they have each chosen the same book (or other piece of literature) to read and study. The children read the chosen piece of literature on their own and then they cluster together to discuss what they feel, know, or want to know about the story and its elements. The teacher reads the same piece of literature and is a member of the group. The group's meeting schedule is determined by their needs: Some read small sections of the book and meet daily, while others may read larger chunks and meet every other day. The specifics of literature group study are discussed in depth in Part II of this book.

The group rules are set by the group and are usually very simple. Each reader comes to the literature group having read the agreed-upon amount and having written personal reactions in a log or journal. Every group member has the opportunity to share their reactions to the text as well as their reactions to the other members' interpretations. The normal rules of group interaction apply; here are some rules my groups have come up with over the years:

- *Speak when you have the opportunity without speaking over someone else.*
- *Share ideas in a positive manner.*
- *Disagree without being disagreeable.*
- *Be courteous, polite, and use good manners when speaking.*
- *Maintain eye contact when speaking.*
- *Be attentive when being spoken to.*
- *Be accepting and respectful of each other; we are all here to share thoughts and ideas.*

feel comfortable enough with their peers to share parts of their life experiences. They talk about real issues sparked by the literature. Debating both sides of an issue leads to well-rounded discussions and new insights.

The Joy of Reading

Literature opens the window to reading enjoyment. Good literature invites children to read a story in its entirety and become involved in an activity that promotes joy as well as learning.

One of my favorite teaching memories reflects the joy one student felt in reading real literature. This student always had a book in his hands. One day as I was passing his desk, I noticed that he had a lap full of books. When I asked about his messy desk, he assured me that his desk was in complete order, but that it was too small to hold his books. Since all the desks were exactly the same size, I bent down to see why his desk couldn't contain all his books. His desk was in order, but it was overflowing with books! He had all the usual fourth-grade supplies along with six library books! Two of the books were from the school library, and the other four were on loan from the public library. Four of the books protruded halfway out of the desk and onto his lap. My first impulse was to

Insights Emerge Through Dialogue

Conversation is the most natural way to create meaning, according to Peterson and Eeds. When people engage in dialogue, they are constructing meaning in a dramatic way. But it takes time to cultivate a community where children feel safe enough to engage in dialogue. When confidence increases, the group as a whole will feel free to debate issues introduced by the literature. The sense of community within the group allows each member to express personal thoughts about an idea. Real dialogues about literature emerge when group members ask him why he had so many books, but the literature lover in me was thrilled to see the enormous pile. I did ask him why he did not at least return the books he was finished with. He informed me that none of the books was completely finished because he always read at least four books at a time. (As one who reads one book at a time, the idea of simultaneously following four plots, numerous characters, several settings and different times, abundant mood changes, and different tensions completely "shocked" me.) When I recovered enough to ask why he would want to engage in so many stories at the same time, his reply again amazed me. He said that when one story got slow or dull, he began reading another to build the excitement, and then he would return to the slow part in the other books again. What a reader! He was an unusual case, but I do believe that through literature groups all students have an opportunity to experience the same joy of reading.

Accounting for Childrens' Special Needs

Some children may have difficulty sharing with a group of their peers. Some are shy, some are less verbal than others; whatever the reason, I believe it is my responsibility to build within those students the confidence to successfully speak and share their ideas in the group setting, if possible.

I begin by speaking privately to them and reassuring them that at no time will they be forced to share verbally if if they don't want to do so. In place of verbal sharing, I invite them to select an alternative way to express their ideas to the group. For example, they can tell their ideas to me, or another group member, and we can share them with the group.

The student can read his or her literature log to the group, or have someone else read it aloud for him or her. Gradually, and working with other students in the group, I will praise and encourage the reluctant students, to strengthen their self-confidence.

Over time, I will continue to create situations where the shy student might feel safe while sharing. These might include talking to me one-on-one, pairing up with one other student to discuss books, recording responses on a cassette tape and playing it for the group, or any other way that would meet the student's needs.

Literature Groups and Reading for Pleasure

The most common feeling children experience when reading for pleasure is the ability to relate to the literature personally. Children immediately see themselves in every situation that even remotely reminds them of their own lives. The personal relationship between literature and reader is forged when the reader identifies with a character, the plot, an object, setting, or illustration, or any other aspect of the book. Literature groups allow children to discuss and share their thoughts, feelings, and opinions once they see reflections of their own lives in the books they're reading.

More Reasons for Reading "Real Literature"

Literature allows the reader to experience a grand variety of different places and times. As stated earlier, many children have never even experienced a visit to a place as ordinary as a zoo. And for some it is only through books that they might do so. Once a student's prior knowledge and experiences are engaged and enriched by the discussion and activities of the literature

My Philosophy of Reading

It took a long time, but after my years of studying reading, plus my classroom experience, I developed a philosophy regarding children and reading.

I came to believe that:

1. Children learn to read by reading.
2. Reading is a process.
3. Children who sample, predict, and confirm text show effective reading strategies.
4. Reading means making meaning from the text.
5. Each child learns at an individual pace.
6. Children are motivated to read when given a choice of books.
7. Reading to children increases their ability to read.

And I believe that using literature groups is the best way to put my philosophy into practice.

group, literature can begin to open new "windows on the world." There are many different genres, and sampling different types of books can bring its own kind of joy.

By sampling different genres, children can become anyone or anything that they desire. They can sing in an opera, dance as a prima ballerina, live on a mountainside, travel on ships to different countries, experience different cultures, become archaeologists, solve mysteries, or share in any way of life they wish. By reading about characters and lives different from their own, students are challenged to view the world differently. This expanded world view enriches their thinking and extends to all aspects of their learning.

From Humble Beginnings...

Wilbur's transformation of character in *Charlotte's Web* in some ways matches transformations in my life as a reader and a teacher of reading. In the beginning I followed my own method and could see no possible way to improve its already "perfect" state. Several "Charlottes" enriched my life by sharing their thoughts, ideas, and expertise. Their caring actions humbled me by helping me acknowledge that the world of reading held many new and exciting avenues for me as an educator.

Reflections

After some intensive reading, reflecting, and planning, I was ready to take the risk of conducting Literature Study Groups in my classroom. However, three major complications would hinder my efforts in bringing about effective literature study in my classroom.

To begin with, our elementary building was departmentalized for reading. Departmentalization meant that students from other classrooms would make up my Literature Study Groups. How could the shared experiences of the Literature Study Group linger throughout the day, intertwined with every other subject? Since approximately two-thirds of my class had reading class in other rooms, I could not use the literature connections in the other subject areas without repeating the conversations of the literature group. The students leaving the room were so removed and disconnected from the literature experience that much was lost in the reiteration.

The second hurdle related to the first. My fellow teachers and I took turns teaching whole reading groups of high-, average-, and low-ability readers. Such homogeneous grouping resulted in little diversity among the readers in the group. A group of children with similar reading skills did not challenge each other. Much of the time they had similar backgrounds and had encountered similar experiences. Therefore, they all brought similar opinions to the discussion of the book.

When these two dilemmas were resolved through negotiation with the building administrator, and an agreement with my coworkers to try self-contained classrooms, I thought that I had finally reached a new plateau in my career. But I soon realized there was one more essential element in a literature group, and that was a set of books! It was virtually impossible for me to find a set of six or seven books of the same title. On my quest, I borrowed books from the public library, collected books from other elementary school libraries, used bonus points from book clubs, and bought paperbacks from former students. My Literature Study Groups grew from humble beginnings, but despite all the obstacles, I find myself looking back in disbelief that I could ever have taught reading by any other method. But I once did.

— Penny

Chapter 2

Selecting and Collecting Good Books

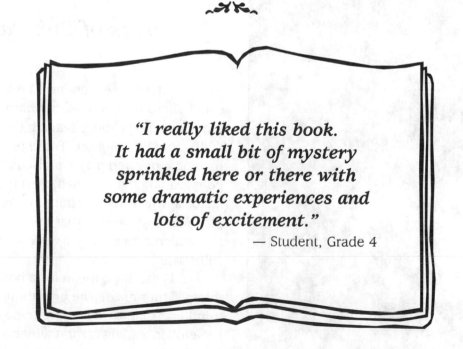

*"I really liked this book.
It had a small bit of mystery
sprinkled here or there with
some dramatic experiences and
lots of excitement."*

— Student, Grade 4

The Bad Book Buy

With my philosophy of reading in place, it was time to begin thinking seriously about my literature collection. It was nearly nonexistent. Those humble literature sets that I had begged, borrowed, and bought were inadequate. I'd need a much larger selection for the number of students assigned to my class and the length of the school year. Clearly, the lack of literature sets was a problem easily solved if the funds were available, but that was not to be my biggest concern. I quickly learned that the quality of the books was more important than the quantity.

At a local bookstore, I bought six copies of what, based on the jacket copy and title,

appeared to be a mystery book with a good plot. Having never read it, I stayed two chapters ahead of the children to be prepared for discussions that took place during the Literature Study Group sessions. I love a good mystery, and I remember my thoughts as I read the book. I kept wondering when the mystery would emerge as I plowed through the chapters. The students anticipated a mystery just as I did, but unfortunately it never materialized. Each of the group members, including me, expressed disappointment. We were all very disturbed with the author and the information on the cover that had lured us into expecting a great mystery. The children were disappointed, and I learned a valuable lesson. Building a library of children's literature is an extremely important endeavor, not to be taken lightly. This was going to be a major undertaking, and I would need to search for recommendations by experts in the field of children's literature and other well-read people.

Books of Substance

After that experience, I realized that I could afford to spend neither hard-to-come-by funds nor the precious reading time of my students on poor literature. Poor literature leads to mediocre or inferior group discussions. Besides, poor reading material had been the deciding factor in my using literature in the first place. I planned to make sure that I never again offered my students another book that was lacking in substance.

What did it mean for a book to be a thing of substance? The only thing that came to mind was that it would have to be sad. I remember reading favorite literature aloud to my students in previous years and thinking, "Why did the dog have to die?" or "How will I read this without letting my voice break with emotion?" (Showing students your emotions is not bad, but it does make it difficult for students to feel the emotion of the text when the teacher is reading in broken spurts and sniffling throughout the tense section of the story!) All books of substance make us think. They do not necessarily have to be sad, but they need to have some "meat" to them that will spark the readers' thoughts and reactions. They are the books that children remember for a lifetime. Sometimes they are the books that change your life or strengthen the ideals you already have.

To me, books of "substance" possess the strength and quintessence of life. Such books contain some characteristic that lingers in the mind of the reader for a lifetime. Some examples of poignant or moving books are *Tuck Everlasting*, *Call It Courage*, *On the Far Side of the Mountain*, *A Wrinkle in Time*, *Island of the Blue Dolphins*, and *Number the Stars*. As a teacher and reader, I had become selective. It was no longer a matter of getting sets of the same books for the study groups. It was now a matter of getting only good literature to put into the hands (and minds) of a group of readers.

Known Authors

I began building a literature library with books by familiar children's authors. Wright, Sachar, Babbitt, Howe, Sperry, Speare, George, Paulsen, and Cleary are just a few familiar authors who have written popular children's books. Those authors, who had been my favorites for read aloud books, were the most logical writers on which to build the foundation of literature in my classroom. I have continued that practice. Every month in book catalogs, the children and I still look for new releases of those special authors we all enjoy.

Each year the students build an Author's Scrapbook. The students fill a three-ring binder with information on authors such as their personal background, their hobbies, and how they get their ideas for books. Children keep a com-plete list of the titles written by each author and a photograph if it is available.

The scrapbook is a valuable resource for the children.

- It allows students to get to know the author in a personal way.
- It provides a resource from which students can choose a book.
- It helps students get ideas for their own stories.
- It provides a way for students to become familiar with authors, adding insight into their reading.

Book Reviews

I find book reviews to be a good source to consult before reaching a decision on purchasing new literature. Reviews by experts in the field of children's literature give a good idea of what new selections are available and provide insight into the quality of each. Book reviews keep me from becoming overwhelmed by the enormous number of children's books that continually become available.

Based on information from reviews, you can order the books of your choice. Another option is to list those books that appeal to you and visit a local bookstore for more comprehensive consideration. Book reviews allow you to scrutinize each literature selection without having to read it first. Many available reviews serve as time management tools for teachers.

Book reviews are available from many different sources.
- Booklist Review
- *Bowker Best Books for Children*
- Bulletin of the Center for Children's Books
- Children's Book Review Service
- The Elementary School Library Collection
- *Horn Book*
- International Reading Association
- Kirkus Reviews

- *Library Journal*
- *School Library Journal*
- *Wilson Children's Catalog Elementary Recommendation*

Recommendations

Another way to select good literature for the classroom is to seek recommendations. You can ask the advice of others, or merely keep your ears attuned to the latest literature. Adults and children alike make literature recommendations. I consider endorsements from each to be equally important, because they are looking at literature from different perspectives. Readers of different ages provide a broader review of the literature.

What Adults Say

Adult recommendations are a great source for locating good children's literature. There are many places to locate adults who are willing to share book endorsements. Excellent sources are the school librarian or the children's librarian of the public library. They work constantly to update their collections and read and critique current books that come onto the market.

Because they are familiar with children's taste in literature, they are expert judges of the different types of literature available.

I have found my colleagues to be quite knowledgeable on literature selections. Working as closely as we do, we have a collective opinion about the types of literature that interest our students and enrich the theme studies in our school. We share new literature discoveries throughout the year.

Share-Time Among Adult Colleagues

Most of the share-time among my colleagues comes in the form of informal chats. We laugh about meeting at the water fountain to make all of our important decisions. We have about twenty minutes to talk at lunch, and our time after school is consumed by meetings and professional growth workshops (not to mention LIFE!) We usually talk about literature when we see each other throughout our busy day.

My colleagues and I are very mindful of the need for good literature that will enhance our themes for the year as well as meet the emotional needs of students. Whenever we find a new book title in a book order, we share our discovery with the teacher it would benefit.

In the spring, we try as a staff to get together and examine our literature collections. This usually occurs in groups of the same grade levels.

The teachers at each grade level discuss the existing book collections and decide what new literature needs to be added. Many of our teachers visit book warehouses to examine the new literature first hand. We travel in large groups down the aisles of bookshelves so we can help each other. I believe we choose the best of the new literature on the market because of the close teamwork generated by these trips.

What Children Say

By far, the best recommendations come from students. They are in a constant state of literature research. Children fill their days with reading, which allows them to become experts in distinguishing good literature from poor literature.

In my classroom, I have found children to be the most valuable resource for reading, digesting, and critiquing a new book. I first began using students as literature critics when I realized that I did not have time to read each book that I wanted to investigate before I purchased it. So I typed a short form for readers to fill out after they had read a book (see page 20.)

Children are uncompromising when it comes to picking good literature. They are completely honest about a book's attributes. They give their honest opinions, because the knowledge that the book could become a literature selection in our library and classroom empowers them to make responsible book critiques.

Because they take their role as book critic seriously, children use the information on each of the Literature Book Critique sheets to create a classroom book review publication. Imitating the ones published in their book orders, children provide a look into new books for all their friends to read. This allows each member of the class to participate in the literature selection process.

Choosing Literature to Enrich Theme Studies

For several years, my classroom literature was chosen strictly through the approaches described above. But after implementing theme studies into the curriculum, I began to find merit in offering books to children that corresponded with the theme being researched in the classroom. When students researched a topic in a content area and then read a piece of literature related to the same subject, they seemed enlightened by the dual learning experience. It also enriched their research and brought a much deeper meaning to the theme being studied. I began to see students applying to the literature the knowledge gained from their research. Consequently, I began to put together literature sets that would enhance each theme being studied. As the literature and the theme began to support each other, I noticed a change in the literature study. While completely absorbed in a theme study of the ocean, one Literature Study Group was reading *Call It Courage*. In the story, Mafatu finds the skeleton of a whale. The following is an excerpt from a student's literature log. The brief passage shows a child's connections between the information collected from the theme study research and a piece of literature about the same topic:

> "Wow, I wonder what kind of whale Mafatu found on the beach. If he knew a lot about whales, he could have identified it. I'll bet it beached itself. That movie we saw on whales said they do that and no one knows why. I'm sure that Mafatu's people knew that because they were islanders and were probably very familiar with whales."

This entry is a sample of the kinds of literature log entries I began to see from children when the literature topic matched the theme topic. It was very exciting, and so I continued

Literature Book Critique

Name of Book _Seabird_
Author _Holling Clancy Holling_
Number of Pages _62_

1. What is the main theme of the book?

   The Sea

   Give a short summary of the book.

   This story, is about an ivory gull, passed on, generation after generation, for more than a century!

2. What is your opinion of the book?
   (Was it easy or hard to understand? Would you recommend it to a friend? Did it remind you of any other books?)

   I loved it! Some of it was hard to understand, but it was great! Yes, I would recomend it to a friend, but it didn't remind me ∗ of

3. Did the book contain any inappropriate parts? (please explain)

   No, It didn't. But I didn't like the part about skinning whales!

4. On a scale of 1 -10 (ten being the best), how would you rate this book?

   I would give it a 10 or 9

5. Do you think this book would be good to use in a literature study group? Why?

   Yes, because it would keep the group intrested! The group would be thankful, for such a book!

the practice with each new theme. Finding quality literature to match the topics of the theme studies was surprisingly easy.

Without any prompting, one of my students approached me one day with a lovely discovery. Ashley said, "Mrs. Strube, I love the book I'm reading for literature group. It is so exciting that I don't want to put it down. Is that how you feel when you read a good book?" My response to her was a resounding "Yes," but my joy went much deeper. All the time and effort I'd put into selecting the best literature for my class had been worth it. Ashley had expressed enthusiasm for reading. The diligent searching for the best literature selections had just been awarded the highest honor possible. A child had found real pleasure in reading good literature, joy that she would keep and share with others for her lifetime.

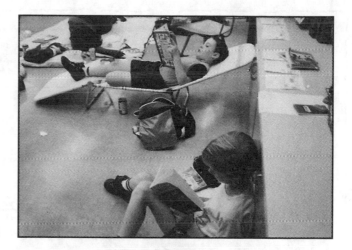

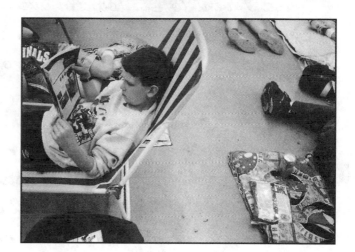

Reflections

I just spent a long, dirty day scouring a book warehouse for the best current literature for my students. My coworkers and I went to St. Louis in two vans and two cars. There were twelve of us. We helped each other search the tall, dusty shelves for those priceless works of literature that will be exactly right for our students.

We found many new titles written by some familiar and favorite authors. I found many new titles on the subject of the Civil War. Fifth grade will be able to use those next year. I had difficulty finding good literature on endangered animals. Endangered animals is such an important issue today, yet it seems very little about them is being written for children.

Yet, it was a very successful day! We spent a great deal of our textbook money, but we have purchased a variety of new materials that will enhance our curriculum in the coming year. The literature hunt binds us together as a community of professionals sharing and caring about each other. The literature will bind children together through Literature Study Groups as they become a community of learners in each classroom and across grade levels. Spending a day with hundreds of works of literature is very inspiring, and today was such a day. In the words of Helen Keller, "Literature is my Utopia."

— Penny

Chapter 3

When Children Choose Literature

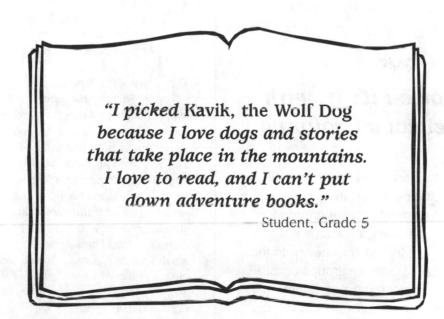

"I picked Kavik, the Wolf Dog *because I love dogs and stories that take place in the mountains. I love to read, and I can't put down adventure books."*

— Student, Grade 5

Choice

Choice is vital to a successful Literature Study Group. When children choose books they are interested in reading, they *will* read them. Choosing their own books encourages them to assume ownership of their decisions and take responsibility for their own learning. Children should choose a book because they're interested in it, rather than because the level of difficulty seems exactly right.

I believe that the issue of whether a book is too easy or too difficult is secondary to a personal decision made out of interest. The art of making a wise book choice isn't innate. It may mean learning strategies that will improve the child's ability to choose books that will challenge his or her reading abilities (see sidebar). This takes slightly more work than the practice of assigning pre-chosen leveled books to homogeneous groups, but the results are worth it.

How Choice Fits in with Heterogeneous Grouping

Because my literature groups are self-selected through children's literature choices, they are naturally heterogeneously grouped. That is, membership in the group does not depend on reading ability but on interest in the book being read. Because these groups consist of children with a range of abilities, talents, and curiosities, they have a perfect opportunity to share diverse experiences with peers. This diversity brings a special richness to the Literature Study Group, and literature is also instrumental in revealing diversity among the readers. The various reading abilities of children in the group

Strategies for Choosing Books Wisely

I try to use questioning strategies and the analogy of the library when I'm explaining how to choose a book wisely. By inviting students to 'turn the situation around' and use their prior knowledge, I find they realize that they have the strategies for picking good books already 'inside them.' I ask them the following questions and get these common responses.

1. *When you go to the library to get a book, what do you do first?*
   "I go to my favorite section like planets or sea creatures."
2. *What if you want fiction?*
   "I go to an author I like or to the award section."
3. *What do you do when you get to that section?*
   "I take out a book that has an interesting title or cover."
4. *Then what do you do?*
   "I open the book and look at the words and read a little."
5. *Why do you read some of the words?*
   "It tells me how hard it is to read, and it helps me decide if I will like the story."

Then I say something like:
"Some of the same strategies apply when choosing a book for class. Begin by choosing a book that contains a theme that you are interested in reading. Picking a book that you like that meets your needs is probably the most important element of choice.

Open the book and read a small section. Decide if the vocabulary seems too simple or too difficult. Either of those two extremes would be a poor choice. From the small section you read, do you think this author will hold your attention? Pick up your second choice and think about the same questions you asked yourself with the first book. Continue this process until you have examined all of the literature choices offered. Then list your top three choices."

contrast sharply with the traditional high, middle, and low reading groups. I once would have thought that this diversity would have negative effects on the children's comprehension, but several experiences changed my mind.

❦

"Chewing the Fat"

My favorite anecdote that illustrates the way diversity strengthens the reading abilities of the entire class is a story about a mainstreamed EMH student who participated in my literature study class for the entire year. She was always excited about joining my class for reading, but because her abilities were low, she was very quiet when the group shared their thoughts about the book.

One day another member was sharing his thoughts about the book the group was studying. He was telling the group that he couldn't figure out what the author meant when he said that some older men were sitting around "chewing the fat." The rest of the group members agreed that the phrase stumped them also. The mainstreamed student softly spoke up and said, "I know what that means." Like any teacher in this situation, you know how it feels to want a child to be right at that moment. I was thinking, "Please let her be right," when she said, "That just means that they were sittin' around talkin'. My grandpa says he's goin' to chew the fat with his friends all the time." I was ecstatic about her answer being correct about the way the author was playing with language. I praised her insight instantly and excitedly went on to explain that this was an expression with a special meaning, called an idiom. She was so proud to be an active part of the literature group. None of the other students had that kind of language experience in their background. She brought a very special kind of diversity to our class that enriched everyone.

How Heterogeneous Grouping Enhances Understanding

When reading Charlotte's Web, *for example, the reader who actually lives on a farm can give insight into the personalities of the animals. True stories about farm life can enhance the fiction. Similarly, students who belong to clubs and organizations that spend time in the wilderness share real-life experiences that mirror the events described in the book* On the Far Side of the Mountain. *When readers have experienced in real life what is being described by literature and can share it with the group, it enhances the literature for all group members. That's why I strive for heterogeneous grouping: to get a greater variety of children, which increases the pool of prior experiences and enriches learning for all of us.*

The very next time her Literature Study Group met, a member had come across another idiom in their reading. After explaining what it meant to the group, he said, "But Mrs. Strube, I forgot what you said this was called." I then asked if anyone in the group could remember the name for this use of language. No one in the study group could. Then from across the room, one student said, "Mrs. Strube, I know I'm not in that group, but I remember what you called it." I was thrilled to realize that while each study group was sharing, the rest of the students were listening to the discussions. Wholeheartedly, I embraced his willingness to contribute his answer. He replied, "You said it was called an idiot." Well, so much for the power of literature study by eavesdropping from outside the group!

Facilitating Choice Through Genre Brainstorming

The first item on my agenda as a facilitator of choice is to brainstorm with children the types of books they would enjoy reading. Before we narrow it down to a title, I like to discuss their preferences of genre. We discuss many different kinds of literature, including: poetry, mysteries, adventure, nonfiction, humor, historical fiction, and personal conflicts. At times we have even discussed authors and then decided to study the different works of one particular author. An author study discussion is productive in a whole group situation, in a small informal group, or individually. In a small group setting, students feel more at ease and readily tell why they are interested in a certain type of book. This interaction may even entice some students to venture into a new type of book after hearing how another child feels about it.

Selecting Literature Sets for Students to Choose From

The brainstorming session guides the teacher to the kinds of literature children are interested in. If students are familiar with authors, they may even name a specific title they might like to read. Several authors have sequels and trilogies that children wish to read next. The selection process then moves to the library, where I spend a great deal of time choosing the selections that students requested. There are several factors to consider when making the selections, some of which are discussed below.

Talking About Genres and Story Elements

In order to discuss genre, I bring in samples I'm sure my students are familiar with. An example of each type of genre that students might choose would be on hand (e.g., humor, historical fiction, mystery). As they name types of books, I have access to one that can exemplify that genre. Children share their reasons for picking a particular genre.

During the Literature Study Group meetings, I present mini-lessons, which deal with specific genres and story elements provided by the chosen piece of literature. Story elements are explored during each study group meeting. If students do not recognize a specific element that is dominant within the assigned reading, I bring it out at the end of the class time.

When we studied James Howe, children went through the usual process of creating groups of four to six members, each to read a different James Howe title: Bunnicula, The Celery Stalks at Midnight, Howliday Inn, Nighty-Nightmare, *and* Return to Howliday Inn.

Students discussed the different literary elements of SETTING, EVENTS, CHARACTER TRAITS, PROBLEMS, and SOLUTIONS.

When each group had completed their book, we formed new groups. The new groups contained one representative from each of the five former groups. Each of the new groups created a chart where they could record all their group comparisons. These comparison charts were displayed for the whole room.

Encouraging Children to Expand Their Choices

I had an avid "horse" reader. Her family boarded horses, so her daily life was infused with the grooming, feeding, and exercise of these animals. Because her personal life revolved around horses, her reading life also centered on them completely. I tried often to show her the merit of different genres yet always failed to coax her away from her preferred reading matter. Then one day, one of her friends in the classroom shared an exciting mystery book that he was currently reading for pleasure. My horse reader went to the library and got a copy so they could share in the same story. She had found a new genre, but not because of my influence. The influence came from a peer. Peer influence is as powerful in the child's world of reading as it is in the adult's world.

More Literature Selection Considerations

Many other considerations factor into the selection process. Some are listed below.
- The genres desired by students
- Books that contain the ingredients for serious contemplation
- The number of groups that will be formed
- The reading abilities of students (less able to highly proficient)

You'll find others, too, I'm sure. In my classroom, I try to facilitate four Literature Study Groups at a time. So six sets of literature are chosen to accommodate the selection process. The sets are checked out, and the excitement begins.

Book Shares

The specifics of the "book share" presentation include a brief summary of the plot, some character introductions, background for the setting, and information about the author and illustrator.

Ways to spark student interest:
- Bring objects to the presentation that will give a concrete understanding of something in the story. (Quilt, coral, an animal, etc.)
- Take a field trip to a related setting. (florist, farm, zoo, etc.)
- Have a guest speaker share their expertise on a book theme. Perhaps they could share slides, movies or materials they have on the book's subject.
- Have a student from another grade come into the classroom and share about the books.
- Play author cassette tapes in which the authors speak about their work.

Finally:
Presenting the Books

This is a fun time for me as an introducer of literature. I feel a lot like the characters in *The Little Red Hen*. I didn't write the books, I didn't illustrate the books, I didn't publish the books, but I certainly read them and loved every minute. That is exactly what I share about the books as I present them to children. I like to shroud the whole book presentation process in mystery and anticipation. I sneak the books in while children are out of the room and put them behind my desk. I even mention that the books are in the room and ask children to please refrain from looking behind my desk. I love to arouse their curiosity about the upcoming literature selections. Children watch the clock.

When the time arrives, I begin the "book share." One at a time, I gingerly lift each book up for the whole class to view as I begin talking about its specific merits. Just the right amount of shared information whets students' appetites, and then I lift another book from behind the desk and begin to share. This continues until all six choices have been presented. The process is exhilarating for both them and me. I invite you to try this or any other method that seems appropriate for "sparking" student interest.

Book Look

The books are arranged on a long table, and each child looks closely at them. They begin to browse through the books, looking for one that appeals to their personality and reading tastes. Children need to choose books that will satisfy their personal needs. Don Holdaway says that wise decisions about choosing books must

be learned, because children do not innately understand the process (*Independence in Reading*, Heinemann, 1980). While children engage in the Book Look, my role is akin to that of the knight guarding the Holy Grail in the Indiana Jones

movie. I move from student to student and engage each in a conversation about the way he or she is choosing a particular book. Then I can utter that much-sought-after expression, "You have chosen wisely." Individual desires and abilities make "choosing wisely" personal and different for each child.

Making a "wise choice" about a book does not necessarily mean that children should pick a book that is on their level of ability. If a less able reader chooses a difficult work of literature, you can compensate for any anticipated reading difficulty in several ways:

- Have paired reading with another group member.
- Other teachers (Learning Disabled, Remedial Reading) can be part of a support team.
- Parents can do shared reading at home.
- Use book tapes (not just store-boughts; they can be made by proficient readers).

Children need to know that if they are interested in a book, regardless of the level of difficulty, I will find a way to facilitate their reading and allow them to find success in their choice.

❧❦

One Child's Courage

Before I began teaching with literature, I held fast to the premise that children should read only material that corresponded with their tested reading ability or level. But as it usually happens, a child, through example, changed my mind and my philosophy. Hannah loved books, but her ability to read was limited. Immediately after the Book Look, she came to me and said, "Mrs. Strube, I really want to read *Call It Courage*, but I think it is too hard for me. But I really, really want to read it, because I love stories about the ocean and sharks."

In my opinion, she was right about the level of difficulty, but I didn't have the heart to tell her she couldn't read it. So she and I set up a system whereby she could read every other page with a friend. As I observed the paired reading, I could tell the friend was getting frustrated with the time it took Hannah to read the page. The friend was gracious and didn't complain, but I knew we needed a backup plan.

I called Hannah's mother and explained the situation, and she agreed to help read at home. The more we got into the book, the more convinced I became that I should not have allowed Hannah to get involved in reading a book that was too difficult for her. That is, until the day she shared her insight about the relationship between the character and herself.

I was keeping anecdotal notes. When she began to speak, I wrote her statement verbatim. She said, "You know how it feels to go diving at the community swimming pool? Well, I think I know what real courage is. It's like when you climb the high dive. If you can swim and you jump off, it doesn't mean anything. But if you are very afraid of heights, and you can't swim very well, and then you jump off the high diving board, that is courage." She was exactly right. Courage reveals itself through acts that provoke fear in the person acting courageously. Hannah's insight was one that no other member of the group had shared, or even considered. Although she had read only a few of the pages on her own, the deep meaning of the book had not eluded her. She taught me a valuable lesson. Interest is the number one driving force behind the desire to read, and making meaning from the story is of the utmost importance.

Choosing Books by Written Ballots

At the beginning of each school year, I find a common problem among my students as they pick a book for the first few times. Because not all are confident in their individuality, they can be swayed easily by well-meaning friends who encourage them to make the same book choice as themselves. So until each child feels confident enough to make wise choices on his or her own, I try to avoid the peer pressure by using the secret ballot.

Using a secret ballot seems to help ward off some of the peer pressures that exist before students become a community of learners. I am not going to tell you that this is completely foolproof, because my previous students have taught me otherwise. Children are so resourceful!

Even though I have spent time encouraging them to make their choice based solely on what they are interested in and not on the reading desires of a friend, I have seen nonverbal signals that are a form of art. Among a few of the best are coded eye blinks, hand sign language that is nothing short of shouting silently across the room, and subtle bidding signals that would make the art world proud. But as children grow in their confidence that reading has meaning in their lives, they are less likely to allow their friends to influence their choices. After they reach that point, the influence of the friend is considered as just one part of a wise decision.

To take the ballot, I invite students to take a small piece of paper and number it from one to three. They then write the name of the books that they wish to read next to the numbers in order of preference. When this task is accomplished, the ballots are put in a jar.

How the Ballots Help in Forming Literature Groups

The names of all six literature selections are displayed on the overhead projector, chalkboard, or dry marker board for the whole class. One at a time, I draw a slip of paper from the jar and write the child's name next to the chosen book title. This is another place where negotiation must occur. Because I believe that a literature group sacrifices its closeness when there are more than six members, I "close" the book as a choice once six readers have chosen it. If a seventh child choses a closed book title as her first choice, I give her the second choice on the ballot. Always, when the child does not receive the first choice on the ballot, I offer to bring the book back the next time we select literature for groups, or I offer to get a copy for the child's personal reading pleasure.

The Power of Choosing

Freedom of choice is a privilege at any age. Along with privilege comes responsibility. Choosing literature out of personal preference and desire encourages children to become aware of the importance of choices in their daily lives.

They are choosing different people, places, and things to read about. These choices allow children to step in and out of wonderful worlds filled with unique people and situations never before experienced in their own lives. I emphasize the importance of choice, because the power of story plays such a significant role in a child's life. What children learn about the world so often comes chiefly from the books they choose to become acquainted with. So choice is vitally important.

Reflections

A few years ago, I was invited to visit a small school district where teachers were eager to change their reading instruction. We discussed the many facets of literature study. Shortly after my presentation, I was preparing to leave for school one morning when the phone rang.

At the other end of the long distance call was a frantic voice explaining that she had attended the inservice on literature study. She had then incorporated literature study into her classroom, and it wasn't working. She was not unpleasant, just desperately in need of assistance to correct the problem. "Just tell me how to make them read the pages assigned for the study group," she pleaded. My mind was swimming! I had never had that problem. I asked if I could take her phone number and call her back after school. Her reply was, "No, I need to know, or I'm not going to be able to face the class during reading time." Grabbing a scrap of paper, I asked her to tell me everything that took place as she initiated Literature Study Groups in her room. My intention was to jot down items as she went along that could be possible solutions to the problem. There was no need for the paper because her first words became permanently etched in my mind. She said, "Well, I went to the library and picked four sets of books and assigned each child to a book, according to their reading ability. Then I told each group how much to read for the next day." I couldn't believe my ears.

Was that how I had presented literature study to her district? I certainly didn't think so— I emphasized to her on the phone that the very first and most essential element of literature study is choice. That was the answer to all her problems.

– Penny

Chapter 4

First
Group Session

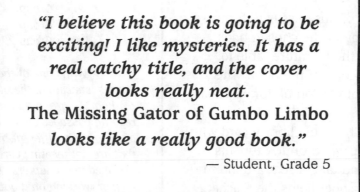

*"I believe this book is going to be
exciting! I like mysteries. It has a
real catchy title, and the cover
looks really neat.*
The Missing Gator of Gumbo Limbo
looks like a really good book."

— Student, Grade 5

Getting Started

The first group session ultimately sets the tone for the complete book study. All the members are equals in the sense that none of them has read the book chosen by the group. So they are embarking upon an adventure with their peers. Their first encounter as a group is the perfect opportunity to create a nonthreatening atmosphere, where children can feel free to state their opinion of the literature.

The Literature Study Group is a community of learners brought together by their common interest in a book. For whatever reason they chose the same work of literature, they will now spend time sharing their thoughts and feelings as a group. The first session gives members an opportunity to bond by discussing their choice.

Assigning a Copy

The first order of business is to furnish each reader with a copy of the chosen book. Each group gathers at the literature table to receive their personal copy of the book. This scene resembles a mini version of library check-out time.

For each book I make a library card with the book copy number typed on it. Students sign the card, file it, and take a seat around the table. A simple record sheet helps the teacher keep track of each student's book number in case the book is lost or misplaced (see page 35 for a sample record sheet).

Classroom Management Tip: Managing Meeting with Groups

The first group session is short compared to the study group meetings thereafter. The initial session provides an opportunity for the group to meet, get books, and make predictions.

Each group meets separately with me at a designated time. We have a specific place in the room where there are three small trapezoid-shaped tables placed together to form a large, somewhat-circular table, which we call the 'lit table.' We have all our group studies at the lit table. The group rules are discussed at the first session of the year. When the readers come for group study, they need to bring their Lit Log, their book, and a pencil. The same rules of being polite, taking turns speaking, and disagreeing nicely still apply.

The regular group sessions are anywhere from 30-45 minutes daily. With four groups, I rotate two groups a day. Every other day, two groups meet. On the posted schedule (see sample on page 39) the groups meeting have an asterisk by their names. For example:

* 1)   *Group 4*
* 2)   *Group 3*
  3)   *Group 1*
  4)   *Group 2*

While one of the two designated groups is meeting, the other students are reading. The group that is up next can be re-reading passages or reading for pleasure out of an entirely different book. The two groups that are not meeting can be reading the assigned new chapters, writing in their Lit Log, or working on a book-related activity with other group members. The room is not noisy because the majority of children are reading. Those who are working on a group activity are very aware of the need for whispering. They are never allowed to disturb the group that is engaged at the lit table.

Book Check-Out Record Sheet

Group 1 - *"Roll of Thunder,*
Hear My Cry"

Copy 1 - *Hannah*

Copy 2 - *Bryce*

Copy 3 - *Allan*

Copy 4 - *Keisha*

Copy 5 - *Nate*

Copy 6 - *Ethan*

Copy 7 - Teacher's Copy

Group 2 - *"Tuck Everlasting"*

Copy 1 - *Romy*

Copy 2 - *Kylie*

Copy 3 - *Sharon*

Copy 4 - *Julio*

Copy 5 - *RoseAlba*

Copy 6 - *Wylie*

Copy 7 - Teacher's Copy

Group 3 - *"Call It Courage"*

Copy 1 - *Ralph*

Copy 2 - *Henry*

Copy 3 - *Nelson*

Copy 4 - *Janice*

Copy 5 - *Heather*

Copy 6 - *Tasha*

Copy 7 - Teacher's Copy

Group 4 - *"The Cay"*

Copy 1 - *Kim*

Copy 2 - *Liza*

Copy 3 - *Jaime*

Copy 4 - *Lamont*

Copy 5 - *Jian*

Copy 6 - *Virginia*

Copy 7 - Teacher's Copy

Prereading Strategies for Creating a Risk-Free Environment

Although the children in each group have been members of a self-contained classroom, they are now uniquely bound together in sub-groups because of their taste in literature.

To create a group environment in which members feel free to express their thoughts and ideas, the teacher can invite the group to participate in several pre-reading strategies during the first session.

Strategy 1: Personal Share Time

As a way to build a community of readers in the newly formed group, a "personal share time" works well. Each group member has the opportunity to share his or her reasons for choosing the book. This builds a collective background that the group can begin to draw from. The students' reasons for choosing a particular book might include one or several of the following:

- Favorite author
- Different or favorite genre
- Interest in content area
- Recommendation from a friend or sibling
- Heightened interest from the classroom book share
- Size or shape of the book

If the last item on the list seems unusual, watch the way children handle books of a strange size or with an unusual cover or binding. Children are drawn to books for the same reasons as adults are and I know the size and shape of a book– how heavy or comfortable it will be to hold– often plays a part in my book choice. By the end of the share time, each group member has new insight into the many different reasons for choosing that particular book. Some reasons my students have given include:

- "I picked this book because my brother said it was good. He has *On the Far Side of the Mountain*, and he won't let me read it until I read this one" [*My Side of the Mountain*].
- "The words on the cover don't mean anything to me that makes sense. 'Gumbo' is soup and 'Limbo' is a dance and then 'Missing Gator' doesn't sound right either. The author might as well call it the 'Missing Gator of Soup Dance', but the title made me want to read it."
- "I picked this book because I like animal books."
- "Betty Ren Wright is one of my favorite authors. I wouldn't miss one of her books for anything."
- "I chose this book, because I like books that have wilderness skills in them. This book will match our study of endangered species."

Strategy 2: Making Predictions

Another strategy is to lead students into making predictions about the possible plot, setting, characters, theme, major events, and so on. As each student shares, it becomes clear to the group that not all of the predictions can become a reality in the book. Each student takes a risk by expressing thoughts and ideas that may never materialize in the book, but by doing so the group is laying a foundation for a community atmosphere. Some students play it safe by predicting the obvious, while others venture out and make bold predictions. Those making bold predictions lead the way for the less confident members.

Strategy 3: Discussing the Book Plot

When children share their ideas about the plot, their ideas show their perceptions of the storyline. Because of their limited experience

Modeling Making Predictions

It takes just a little time to teach students how to make predictions. Like many learning strategies, it is modeled and discussed many times throughout the year. I find it helpful to use real-life situations when modeling making predictions. Drawing from experiences they may have seen on t.v. (which most kids consider part of real-life), in a movie, or experienced first hand, we discuss what might happen next in a given situation.

- *A wild horse is captured and desperately wants its freedom. Children predict ways in which the horse will be freed.*
- *A tornado is racing toward a community. Children predict what might happen to the town.*

After predicting what might occur in certain familiar situations, we then move into the events that provide clues in the literature. Children explain their predictions and we record them on a large sheet of paper. As the story progresses, we track the predictions and mark them as they develop. Some predictions do not become a reality in the literature. We just put an X next to those that do not come true.

with literature, most of the plots they envision are simple.

When children begin to share what they perceive the plot to be, they display their knowledge and experience with literature. As they describe possible alternative plots, they share their knowledge of how stories generally unfold and end. These conversations easily spark new avenues for discussion, valuable information about the children and their prior literature experiences. Excitement builds as I realize that what the children expect to occur in the story will not occur. Instead, a new experience in literature awaits them. Sample plot statements:

— "In stories where a child runs away, they usually come back home in the end."

— "When dogs run away or are taken away, they always try to get back to their masters and they always do."

— "Normally when a child runs away, he or she learns what you can or can't do wherever they go."

— "When children run away, people usually send out a search party. In the mountains, they send a helicopter."

These outcomes are not always reflected in the literature students read. Through their prior knowledge of life as they have encountered it in literature, on television, or at the movies, children create possible scenarios for the plot of their new book. This heightens their interest in the literature and helps connect it to real life.

Strategy 4:
Getting Acquainted with the Author

Introducing the author is very important, not only to the children as readers, but also to the children as writers. As the story progresses, the group will discuss the author's purpose, ways of playing with language, and ability to capture the reader's attention. But during this beginning session, just getting to know the author provides insight into the author's style of writing.

Strategy 5:
Discussing the Author

- Author's personal background
- Author's culture or environment
- Author's other works
- Author's style of writing
- Author's favorite genre

This information can be attained from several sources. Book clubs offer materials about authors in various forms. Audiocassette tapes provide information along with authors reading all or part of their work. Biographies have background material about the author's personal life and habits. Authors write letters that give a feeling of closeness and familiarity. Internet correspondence is an exciting technological way of speaking directly and personally to an author.

Strategy 6:
Creating an Author's
Window Flower Box

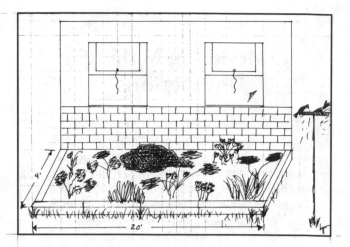

Many strategies promote genuine closeness between authors and readers. One of the most exciting projects in my classroom was the creation of an authors' flower box. The students created a flower box that stretched from window to window on the ground just outside our classroom. The students built the four foot by twenty foot window box entirely on their own. They raised money through a classroom book business, The Book Nook, to buy the landscape timbers. They measured the ground, rolled back the grass, dug small shallow trenches around the perimeter, fitted the timbers into the trenches and covered the dirt with heavy plastic to prevent weeds. During construction of the window box, they gathered information from favorite authors. The children composed a form letter (see sidebar) with room for a handwritten personal touch. Every student sent a letter to a favorite author asking about his or her favorite plant or flower.

❧❧

Ending the First Meeting

After members of the new group have become acquainted by participating in several prereading strategies, it is time to conclude the group discussion. Again, choice plays an important role in decision making. Before children leave the group setting, they need to choose the amount of text they wish to read before they come back together as a discussion group. The group must be in agreement about the number of pages. The number of pages will vary with the age, interest, and type of reader (novice/proficient). Many students vote to read large portions of the book, while others prefer to limit the amount. When given the freedom to choose, students come to a decision that all find acceptable.

Letter to a Favorite Author

Dear _____,

My classroom is building a ground-level window box outside our classroom. We have raised the money through our classroom book business to buy the window box materials. We want to fill it with the preferred plants and flowers of our favorite authors. We hope you will tell us the name of your favorite plant or flower, so we can plant it and make a metal plant label with your name engraved on it. By labeling the flowers, everyone will get to know you a little better.

We love your books and would be privileged if you would write and tell us the name of your favorite plant or flower and why it is your favorite. If you could send us a seed from one of your own plants, it would be great, but if not we will buy one and put your name on it. This project is very important to us, because we think reading is very important.

Thank you for your time, and most especially thank you for writing stories that we love so much.

Sincerely,

_____

Scheduling Literature Group Meetings

I cannot meet every day with each reading group. I meet with two groups every other day to allow longer discussions, and more time for the groups *not* meeting to read and respond to the literature. Reading can take place inside or outside of the classroom. When I meet with the groups, we will be discussing, not reading, so all the agreed-upon pages must be read before we meet. However, the groups I am not meeting with can use the reading period time in class to read or to respond to their reading in their literature logs (see Chapter 6). Daily classroom schedules (sample below) show the title of the book, the meeting time, pages to be read (asterisks denote the groups that will be meeting with me), and which groups will meet that day.

Sample Literature Study Group Schedule

12:30-2:00	Pages
* Group 1 - "Roll of Thunder, Hear My Cry"	(40 - 60)
* Group 2 - "Call It Courage"	(55 - 65)
Group 3 - "Tuck Everlasting"	(30 - 45)
Group 4 - "The Cay"	(70 - 95)

Notes: *Groups 1 and 2 will meet with me to discuss the books they are reading. Groups 3 and 4 will use the time to read the chosen pages in their books or write in their literature response logs*

One of the questions most often asked of teachers is, "After all of the prereading strategies, what do you do if a student decides he/she doesn't want to read the chosen book?" A real-life experience makes this question very easy to answer. When I was in the sixth grade, I chose a book from our room library to read for a book report. I chose Wilder's "The Long Winter." I chose it because of its size. It was huge, and I wanted to read a book that made me look scholarly. After reading a few chapters about relentless hardships, freezing conditions, and a plot centered around children bundled up and confined to their beds for warmth and survival, I decided pioneer life was not for me. I took the book up to my teacher, and asked if I could choose another book. Her emphatic <u>no</u> has lingered with me for a lifetime. She said, "You picked it and you will read it." And read it I did, but I never picked up another book in the "Little House" series until I was an adult. Not only did I avoid that series, I managed to avoid the whole theme of pioneer life. As a child, I lost out on some of the most wonderful literature written. I was afraid to take the risk of choosing another pioneer book, of finding once again that I did not like it and being forced to read it anyway. Because of my personal experience, I allow students to choose another book if they are truly unhappy with a book for valid reasons. If they choose another book, they are responsible for catching up on the reading, so that they can join in and become an active part of the new group.

— Penny

Chapter 5

Independent Reading

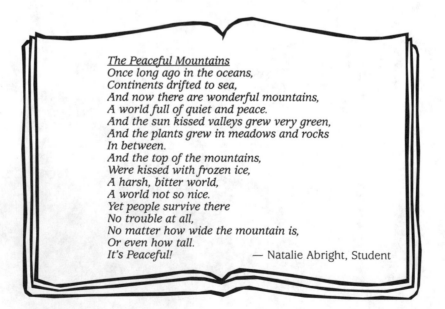

The Peaceful Mountains
Once long ago in the oceans,
Continents drifted to sea,
And now there are wonderful mountains,
A world full of quiet and peace.
And the sun kissed valleys grew very green,
And the plants grew in meadows and rocks
In between.
And the top of the mountains,
Were kissed with frozen ice,
A harsh, bitter world,
A world not so nice.
Yet people survive there
No trouble at all,
No matter how wide the mountain is,
Or even how tall.
It's Peaceful!
— Natalie Abright, Student

Providing Time to Interact with Text

To become meaning makers, children must become actively engaged in reading independently, and it is our goal as educators to facilitate a child's ability to read independently. The realization by Frank Smith that children learn to read by reading reinforces the importance of independent reading time.

Children need "time" to read. Time to journey into a text independently is vital to the success of the Literature Study Group. Children need uninterrupted time to read, think, ponder, and respond to the text. For children to make meaning from the text, they must have time to dwell in the story world with the characters. When given generous amounts of independent reading time, students dive beneath the surface of the story to greater depths of meaning. The author's words penetrate the reader's experiences and bring to life greater understanding from the text. To paint a visual picture of what I mean by "spending time in the text," I discuss the movie *The Neverending Story* with my students. The movie demonstrates the way a reader becomes a character in a story by sharing actions, fears, excitement, and adventure as he or she moves in and out of the text. The movie illustrates how a reader enters, exits, and reenters a story in a dramatic way.

There are many ways to ensure that students receive the extensive reading time they need.

- Schedule daily time for Sustained Silent Reading (SSR).
- Schedule large blocks of reading time. It is so important to have a large block of uninterrupted time for litertaure study and independent reading. Scheduling it can sometimes be a problem, with all the pull-out programs and special scheduled events and activities most schools provide for children. But it is worth trying to build

large blocks of time into your day for reading, because, for some children, these times are the only occasions set aside for reading in their busy day.

- Encourage reading during any free time. As I move through the room working individually with students, I try to encourage those with spare time to read. In our room, a special area with two real ficus

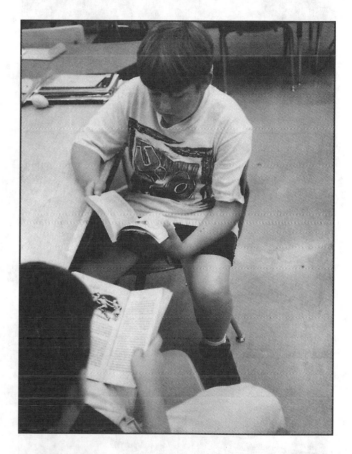

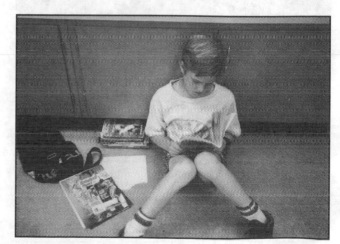

trees, a park bench, a huge aquarium, and our classroom library shelf provides an alternative place for children to read in their spare moments. But any place can be a 'reading place'; decor is not as important as the feeling that 'this is a place and this is the time for me to read.'

- Create home reading programs with parents.
- Plan special reading events (classroom or entire school).
- Set up reading programs with other classrooms (peer reading, big buddy reading).

Sustained Silent Reading

Sustained Silent Reading provides time for every member of the class to read. Everyone in the classroom (including the teacher) reads whatever he or she wishes. The time becomes a treasured event in the daily routine. For fifteen or twenty minutes, nothing takes place in the classroom except peaceful, silent reading for pure enjoyment.

Home Reading Programs

Home reading programs stem from the classroom. Usually the teacher contacts the parents and provides suggestions for home reading. The reasons may be to stimulate reading habits, to promote reading programs offered through businesses or book companies, or to extend the classroom emphasis on reading into the home. When parents get involved in their children's reading, children grow in attitude and ability.

Special Reading Events

Special events can provide the means for more independent reading time. Reading events can take place before, during, or after the school day. Students especially enjoy a read-a-thon. By designating one day as a reading day, children can plan to relax with books all day. Special activities can include having guest readers, visits by authors and storytellers, which give a read-a-thon a dramatic boost. The reading day may consist only of children reading, with intermittent times for the teacher to share a read-aloud book. For a dramatic difference, invite children to bring in blankets, sleeping bags, pillows, lawn chairs, or bean bag chairs. Readers may bring snacks to enjoy while they read. Whether it is a day of special activities or just a day in the classroom lounging and reading, the read-a-thon provides an extraordinary amount of time for children to enjoy the world of reading.

Peer Reading

Another way to provide time for students to read is to have them participate in peer reading. Reading aloud to other children provides a foundation for their own reading. They begin to hear themselves and believe that they are readers. If peer reading occurs with students in or near the same grade level, they take turns reading to each other. Reading to children who are much younger provides the same opportunity for the more proficient reader and helps to secure the sound of story for the novice reader. Both methods of peer reading give children extra time to engage in reading.

Relating Personally to Make Meaning

Reading independently can enable readers to connect what they read to their own experiences. In fact, those connections momentarily impede the reader's flow as a related experience unfolds in the reader's mind. This behavior, where one stops and ponders the memories of life experiences, is commonly labeled "daydreaming."

The author's descriptive language begins to create a mental picture resembling the reader's memory of a familiar setting. Personal recollections create meaning as the story develops. These recollections may take the form of written responses, as the following examples demonstrate.

(Student's written response to The Wolfling by Sterling North)

"When I read how Robbie went fishing for his birthday and caught a few fish, it reminded me of the time I caught my first fish. It wasn't too long ago, just this last summer. My dad had to fix the riding lawn mower down where we used to live, and I got bored after awhile. So I ran to the garage and took out fish food and a net and ran to our pond 100 feet away. I tossed some food in and waited. Then suddenly the pond came alive with the wild splashing of catfish fighting to get some of it. I got ready, then dipped the net in the water. Success! A huge catfish flopped within my net! After I called dad and he clapped, I set it free. In the day I caught one more and let it go too. I was so happy! I caught my first fish!"

Many times, as with this entry, personal connections do not add information or critical value to the story. But by bringing the reader into a closer relationship with the story, the connections become invaluable. Personal connections create meaning between the reader and the text that motivates the reader intrinsically. That intrinsic motivation is the personal desire that keeps the reader reading.

Contemplating New Ideas

While the student reads independently and reacts personally to the literature, other connections begin to emerge. When readers digest new thoughts and ideas brought about through interaction with the text, their reaction to the new information reflects their understanding and feelings as independent readers. That understanding may change when the reader listens to other reactions from the discussion group. These connections may also take the form of journal entries like the following.

(Student's reaction while reading independently)

"I learned about passenger pigeons in these chapters. I learned how they only laid two eggs in a nest of just a few sticks on a limb, and how people who wanted to kill them would put sulfur on bonfires, or use dynamite and shotguns to knock them out of the trees at night! That makes me mad!"

This reader's feelings probably will not change when shared with the literature discussion group. The shocking behavior described in the book resulted in anger for the reader who was previously unaware of these practices. The new ideas made a lasting impression on the reader.

Time Revisited

As we've seen, time is an essential ingredient for independent reading, and it is also essential for thinking. Before, while, or after readers engage in the reading process, they need time to think about the new ideas, feelings, and connections that the story evoked. Time spent weaving together new concepts may appear to the untrained "kidwatcher" as time wasted on daydreams. But daydreaming may be an example of a student making connections. Time spent in deep thought is time well spent.

Reflections

I've discovered one very important influence on the success of independent reading in the classroom: a good role model. If a teacher wants her students to read independently, then she must demonstrate independent reading herself. Lucky for me, I love to read, so it's never a hardship for me to join the students during SSR. For the SSR period, I have the pleasure of getting lost in a story of my choice. Later, I tell the students of my excitement at having the time and opportunity to read independently.

Many times, as I sit reading among my students, I look up briefly to survey the room. A student's eyes meet mine, and I realize that instead of reading her book, she is studying me and my reading behavior. It may be the way I lightly tap my bookmark on my temple, the way my eyes move as I follow the lines of text back and forth across the page, or my habit of quickly turning the page to keep my reading rhythm. Whatever— it seems I give away my love of reading by my body language and mannerisms. I've come to believe that reading with the students encourages them to become better readers. After all, children learn by our example, and I'm confident that in this, at least, I'm setting a good one.

— Penny

Chapter 6

Using Literature Response Logs

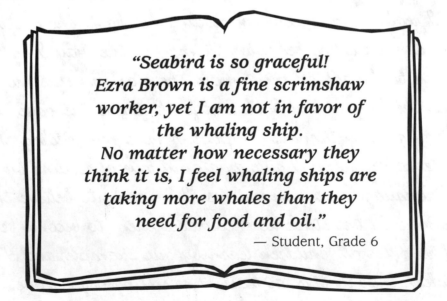

"Seabird is so graceful!
Ezra Brown is a fine scrimshaw
worker, yet I am not in favor of
the whaling ship.
No matter how necessary they
think it is, I feel whaling ships are
taking more whales than they
need for food and oil."
— Student, Grade 6

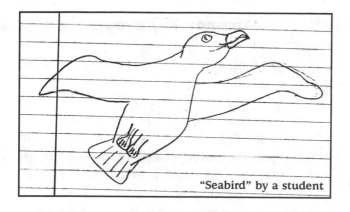

"Seabird" by a student

Why I Use Literature Logs

A literature response log (or "Lit Log" as the children refer to it) is the place where readers record their personal reactions to text. It is where they may document their feelings as they interact with the text, construct meaning, and/or digest their new thoughts, ideas, and connections. Responding to literature in this personal way gives readers control over their experiences with the story. As soon as students have completed reading the agreed-upon number of pages, they respond to the literature by writing in the literature log. Thus, this activity is done every time the literature groups meet after reading.

The log can be used to stimulate group dialogue when used as a beginning point for discussion. Many times children forget all the different parts of the story that they want to discuss unless they have a written record of it. The log provides that written record. It becomes the springboard for individual and group discussion. The focus of the literature group discussion comes from the thoughts the students have begun to explore in their response logs, so that what the students record as they interact with the text will determine the path of their group discussion. For this reason you may wish to help shape their responses by modeling the sorts of responses that will lead to meaningful discussion. I model responses to literature by sharing my own written responses with the students as I meet with them in Literature Study Groups.

Demonstrating Responses

Although children learn by doing, they also need opportunities to observe others who are more experienced than themselves in order to refine their skills. Children improve their abilities to respond to literature by observing teachers as they share their interpretations of a story. It is important to share with students how to build personal meaning into the literature log responses. It is also important for the teacher to write literature responses in a log, just as the students do. Modeling log responses gives the teacher the opportunity to share reading/writing connections with the discussion group.

I model how to respond to literature by keeping a Lit Log of my own. Instead of giving the students specific characteristics to follow, I allow them to respond freely and then I share freely from my log entry. In this way I am modeling, but still allowing for their individual response.

Beginning to Model: Thinking Aloud

In addition to modeling my Lit Log responses (which I discuss in depth in the following pages) at the beginning of a literature discussion group session, I ask the students to observe my actions as I dramatize how I respond to the literature as I read. As I read from the text, I stop and say what would be going through my mind if I were reading silently.

(Excerpt from Tuck Everlasting)

"Winnie had often been haunted by visions" (I wonder why she refers to her thoughts as visions. Most people think of them as dreams or just thoughts) "of what it would be like to be kidnapped." (I remember standing and staring at a picture of a little girl who had been kidnapped. It was hanging on a bulletin board in a grocery store.) "But none of her visions had been like this, with her kidnappers just as alarmed as she was herself." (Maybe they are just nervous because it is their first kidnapping. Whenever you do something for the first time, it can be scary.) "She had always pictured a troupe of burly men with long black mustaches who would tumble her into a blanket and bear her off like a sack of potatoes while she pleaded for mercy." (Now this is the way I think of a kidnapping happening, too. That is the way it is usually portrayed on television and in movies.) "But instead it was they, Mae Tuck and Miles and Jesse, who were pleading." (The author has made this kidnapping very unusual. It doesn't fit any of the usual patterns you see in life. There must be a reason why Winnie is being treated so differently. They seem to be almost afraid of her.)

I stop and share each thought that goes through my mind as I read and "think" aloud to the group. After I "think" aloud, I write that response in my Lit Log. This is a dramatically visual way of demonstrating how thoughts and connections turn into valuable literature responses.

❧

Ways of Responding

There are many ways to respond to literature. Many children initially respond by paraphrasing the events in the story, simply recalling facts rather than reflecting upon them. Teachers can accept this initially, and then help the students grow past this stage. Three of these initial ways of responding to literature follow.

Summarzing Events

Students may summarize story events in Lit Logs, as the following sample shows.

"In these chapters Gillon gives Omri a cupboard. Omri puts the cupboard in his room and puts the plastic Indian in it. Before Omri put the cupboard in his room, he went to look for a key to lock the cupboard. The key that he found was his mum's grandmother's key to a jewel box. In this book Omri calls his mom mum. When Omri puts the Indian in the cupboard, the next morning the Indian is alive."

This shows that the reader is aware of what happened in the story and the sequence in which the events took place. Another student added art as shown in the "Events " list below.

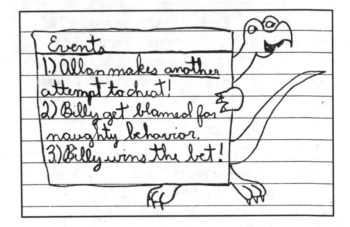

Describing the Setting

Students may use their Lit Log entries to describe the settings.

"This story takes place in Wisconsin, so far. It is in the mid-early 1800's."

From this simple statement, it is apparent that the reader realizes that the setting could change or expand in the story. This shows growth from the stage of belief that setting is an unchanging concept fixed in the beginning of the story.

Identifying Characters

Another Lit Log activity involves having students write about the characters.

"The characters are Robbie, the well-educated boy, Thure, the professor, and a whole cast of other characters so numerous I can't write them down. I think there is more than one main character. I think the main characters are Old Three Toes and Robbie. It's because you hear mostly about Robbie and the timber wolf with only three toes on her paw."

This student has grown from just naming the characters to separating them into main characters with supporting details.

When children begin to expand their reaction to the literature by exploring more story elements, their log entries reflect their new ideas and connections. These expanded reactions are illustrated below.

Illustrating Characters, Settings, and Events

Students love using their Lit Log time to illustrate as well as write about their reading. Illustrations add so much to the log. Children love to show their sketches to the group. "Artistic" merit is not the key value emphasized in evaluating these entries. The value comes from helping the children make meaning from the story through drawing. The illustrations can enhance or explain the students' writing.

The big green wave that swept Bubbles out to sea.

Analyzing Characters

Students may also analyze characters.

"I don't think too highly of Bubs Mooney. First of all, he was sassy to his teacher, Mrs. Hitchcock, who is a very nice lady. He's also, well, not really, um, polite towards Robbie. If I could spend a day with Robbie or Bubs, I'd probably spend the day with Robbie. But I will give Bubs a chance to be a character as likable as Robbie."

The student's views of the characters are remarkably well-developed. The characters have personalities; not just names, ages, and sizes. The log entry demonstrates the voice of the reader (in written form).

Comparing and Contrasting Story Elements

Comparisons and contrasts can be expressed in words, on charts and diagrams, or by illustrations in logs. (Students find many ways to record their thoughts.)

"When I read that the soldiers had to eat soap, hair grease and candles, it reminded me of another thing I read about Ferdinand Magellan. I read that on his long journey, he ran out of food provisions. He and his followers had to eat sawdust found on the ship."

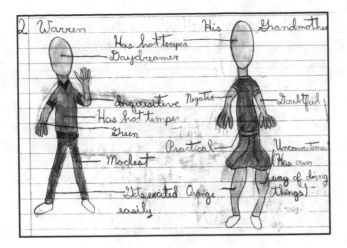

The comparison between the soldiers and Magellan increased the reader's understanding of life's hardships.

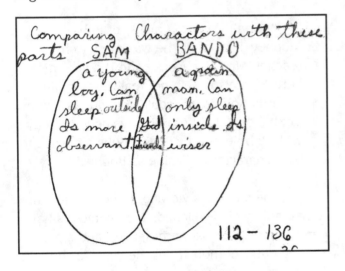

Relating Personally to Story Elements

The following sample shows another type of Lit Log response.

"Pedro reminds me of myself in some ways. Sometimes he's confused about something and asks someone for help. Also, he likes to write, and he is good at it. And one more thing. It took me awhile to learn to swim, too. It is funny how we have so much in common."

The reader related personally to Pedro's life with several memories of similar experiences.

This vivid response could create images others might identify with, thus providing another "way into" the story for group members.

Discovering Relationships

There are many ways to examine relationships. One way is to use cause and effect, and expressing the relationship in a chart as shown below. Charts and drawings are acceptable Lit Log entries.

Cause	Effect
Because Joshua Smith saw C. Livingston in a British uniform while sewing.	He had second thoughts about keeping his job.
Because Major André was caught	he became a prisoner of war and was hanged
Because Arnold was exposed as a traitor	he had to try to explain why he was one.

Describing the Mood

This Lit Log entry tells that the mood is sad, and goes on to tell the circumstances that have caused the mood to be sad.

"This part of the book has been full of sad events. Bummer! The British were winning in the South when the Americans had trouble finding money to pay their soldiers. Benedict Arnold was actually communicating with major Andre' of the British, his enemy, and fed valuable information to the British."

Many times mood is hard for students to describe or explain. The above is the kind of entry readers make as they improve in their ability to express their understanding.

Analyzing Problems and Looking for Solutions

It is easy to see in the following Lit Log entry that the reader has spotted a problem and is searching for possible reasons or causes.

"I don't understand something. I thought Arnold was against the French and hated them. But now Arnold has just "lowered himself" (as he put it) to go to the French Ambassador and ask for a loan! I find that hard to believe. I then read on and found out that he and Major Andre' were communicating. I believe there is a problem here. The problem is that Arnold isn't behaving like a patriot any more. This could cause lots of problems if he turns out to be a traitor."

The next step is to begin to formulate possible solutions.

As the community environment builds in the Literature Study Group, the risk-free atmosphere encourages the readers to stretch their interpretations into higher levels of thinking. Their responses begin to contain thought-provoking ideas. Some students start to feel comfortable sharing their thoughts about the literature, even when these thoughts might be controversial or iconoclastic.

The following literature log entries reveal real growth on the part of the readers to make meaning from the text. The entries share ideas and insights substantiated by detailed reasons. These entries represent the types of responses that teachers can model to help the readers grow into productive and successful meaning makers.

Interpreting the Author's Purpose

One way of making meaning from the text is by attempting to "get inside" the author's mind, as this sample shows.

"I think the author has more than one purpose. First of all, I think she wanted to inform people about historical moments and to use the book as a learning tool. She probably thought it would be a little more informative and easier to learn about black history in a realistic, but fictitious book than a boring article in a social studies book. I also think she wrote it to show the horror black people went through when white people kept slaves. It also tells about the underground railroad, and how some people really did care about freeing the slaves and abolishing slavery. Finally, I think this book means a little more than an informative source or a resource on black history. I also think that it was written to show that people change over the course of their years and sometimes over the course of a month or two."

Predicting Outcomes

Attempting to predict the outcome of the story is another way children use their Lit Logs to make meaning, as this entry shows.

"I predict in the next few chapters that Kurt, Sam and Jeff will go to Padre Island and look for treasure. The author gave some not so subtle hints that they would, like their reaction and choice of words when Sally told them about the treasures and great riches buried in sunken ships on Padre Island."

Composing a Work of Creative Writing

Sometimes the meaning-making extends to creating a new work of art, such as these poems (and illustrations) one student created in her Lit Log.

Ode to Wolf
A wolf is a wolf,
They do like to steal.

And they prove themselves clever,
When it comes to a meal.

by Natalie Abright

War of Independence
Muskets, cannons,
Bayonets,
Were used to fight the war.
Blue and red
The soldiers were
And I am very
Sure.
The British and the
Frenchmen fought
They ripped, they shot
They tore.
The bloodiest battle
ever fought,
The Revolutionary
War.

by Natalie Abright

British
Everyone feared taxes
Nobody thought Benedict would turn out
  good
Every British soldier wore red
Daredevil
Independence
Colonists
Tea

by Natalie Abright

Daisy
Daisy is a humpbacked whale,
With a swish of her flippers
And a swash of her tail,
She's swimming in the open sea,
There she breaches,
That's Daisy!

by Natalie Abright

Critiquing an Aspect of the Book

This sample shows the student's feelings about the author's skill.

"The author did a great job getting me into it! I like how she would write what Warren was dreaming up, like how he would think about two sewer workers eating lunch and when the goldfish would come and suck them up! It was great!

"I liked the illustrations very much. They are so detailed. I'm a bit disappointed that it didn't say who did them. Still a book without illustrations lets you use your imagination more."

Sharing and Supporting Personal Opinions

These interpretations come after the readers become more confident and knowledgeable.

"Right now in the book, I'm mad or angry at some people. I'm angry at Sam because of his attitude problem, which he could change. Even though it's hard on a kid to have a parent who is gone all the time. The second person I'm mad at is the waitress. Sam forgot his billfold of money when he went to the restaurant for steaks. He honestly said he didn't have it, but the waitress snapped at him and said she didn't believe him. Even though she was doing her job, she could have at least checked into things!"

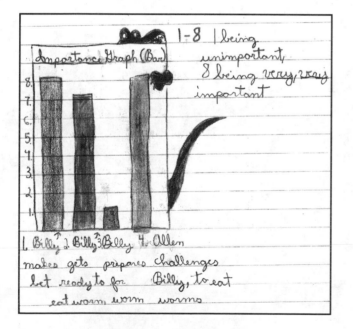

Evaluating Story Events' Importance

The following sample evaluation of story events' importance takes the form of a graphic organizer. Billy's actions are rated on a scale of 1 to 8.

Judging Events and Supporting with Reasons

With each group meeting, we learn from each other, and praise each other's innovative responses, and try to look deeper into the elements of literature. This results in Lit Log entries such as this:

"I thought these chapters were horrible! I can't believe the soldiers crammed everyone into trucks, drove them to the train station, stole their possessions, then crammed them into a boxcar. That is awful! Why would anyone do something like that? It was terrible just hearing about it, but people actually experienced it."

This level of understanding comes through several months of listening as a group to literature responses of others in the group and the teacher. It doesn't happen overnight, but it happens!

❧❦

Using Literature Log Prompts

To help readers develop the ability to respond in a deeper, more thoughtful manner, many teachers provide a list of ideas to prompt the readers' responses. These lists are meant to guide the reader into more stimulating responses, but are by no means commands to be followed precisely, or assigned. They are meant to be used only as a gentle nudge when necessary.

Prompts are usually written as statements or questions on a wall chart or chalkboard. Some samples follow:

- Tell about the story.
- Describe the characters.
- Give your opinion of a character.
- Compare a character in this story to another character you remember in another story.
- How has the main character changed as the story progresses?
- How has the author drawn you into the story?
- What are some of the hidden meanings you are finding?

What Children Say About Literature Study Groups

My beliefs in the value of Literature Study Groups are strengthened by comments, like the following, from students.

— "I get to learn how other people see the story."
— "I love to hear how my friends feel about the story."
— "When I share my Lit Log, I like the way I feel when everyone listens to me."
— "I like to hear about everyone's favorite parts."
— "I like to listen to see if others have the same ideas that I do."
— "It is fun to listen to the stories that my friends tell about their own lives."
— "The questions that everyone asks really make me think about the story."

Reflections

The literature log is more than a security blanket or memory aid for the reader to use when revealing her personal thoughts to the group during discussion. It serves a dual role. First, the literature log is an excellent source of assessment information. In it, the child reveals so much more about her reading abilities than any standardized test ever could. In the Lit Logs, students show their strengths as well as areas in need of improvement to the trained eye of the teacher.

Second, in Lit Logs, students reveal who they are as people when they interpret and react to the events unfolding before them on the page. And they never cease to amaze me!

For years now, I have been privileged to share in the personal, social, and academic revelations that are written within the covers of Lit Logs. I've shared the excitement, sadness, anger and delight recorded by the children I've taught. These children allow me to enter into their world of interpretations and there I feel, like Wilbur, "Radiant."

— Penny

Chapter 7

Literature Study Groups in Action

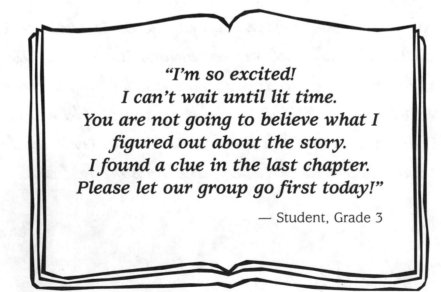

*"I'm so excited!
I can't wait until lit time.
You are not going to believe what I
figured out about the story.
I found a clue in the last chapter.
Please let our group go first today!"*

— Student, Grade 3

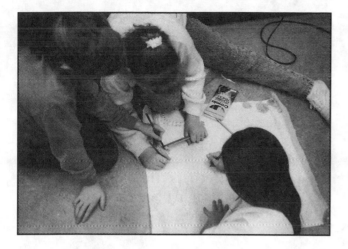

conversation. The log functions as a support for the shy, non–risk taker and as a springboard for the confident, expressive reader. Literature logs provide a place to document special passages that the reader finds meaningful and wants to share with the group. As discussed in Chapter 6, students record in the log thoughts to be discussed and expanded upon by the group. The log is not the end product of the reading experience. Rather, it becomes an artist's pad for demonstrating particular aspects of the story through writing, sketches, illustrations, and diagrams. It serves as a place for the reader to record unanswered questions about the story and exact locations in the book where the text became confusing. The log protects the personal creative pieces generated as the reader interacts with the text. These elements of the literature log create a powerful tool from which each group member draws as together they share their text interpretations.

Preparation for Group Session

The social actions of reading and writing create a bond among the community of learners as members of the Literature Study Group prepare to meet by reading the chosen pages and responding to the text by writing in their logs. I, too, prepare in a similar way.

It is extremely important that the teacher read and respond to the same section of literature as the students. In this way, the teacher is prepared to be an active participant in the literature group. As the group assembles at the table, or designated spot, each member comes prepared to interact with the group by bringing their books and literature response logs.

Real Dialogue

The main purpose of discussing a book is to acquire a thorough and complete understanding of the text. The text is re-entered and explored not by just one reader, but by a group of readers. The goal of the discussion group is to discuss and negotiate meaning, connect and combine ideas, and create new meaning to bring about a greater understanding of the literature. The literature log is a useful support to ensure meaningful discussion.

Using the Literature Response Log

The function of a literature log differs from student to student, group to group, and even teacher to teacher. Depending on the nature of the group as a community, students may read verbatim from the log during discussion time after reading, or simply refer to it to support the

Sharing Information

As children begin to share information, the group uses its prior knowledge to make meaning. They may share personal memories of life events, stories remembered from other books, episodes viewed on television, or action-packed scenes from a new movie as they bond with the group. For example, during a discussion of the book *Jelly Belly*, the following dialogue ensued:

Angela: Ned said that one of the few things he liked about camp was getting mail. I like getting mail for my birthday, because sometimes I get money in it. It is an exciting time when I get mail. I know the campers were excited. They weren't looking for money, though. They were looking for food. The campers finally go to the can of tennis balls. I guess there were goodies or something like that in there.

Teacher: In the can?

Lisa: They took the balls out of the tennis can and stuffed food that they weren't supposed to have down in the can.

Although Angela's personal sharing seemed a small part of the discussion, she reinforces the feelings of happiness and excitement that can be felt when mail arrives. Her thoughts did not alter the direction of the conversation, but they added an explanation of mood.

Revealing Insights

From time to time, children have trouble expressing all their thoughts in a written log. Some ideas need to be explained orally. The literature group gives children the opportunity to describe how they arrived at a conclusion, how they formulated their solution, and how they constructed their new meaning. The following Lit Log entry was further explicated by the discussion below:

"I knew right at once that Sara's dad didn't have a good job. I could tell by the way the author described how depressed he acted about it. That's the way my dad acted until he got a better job. It must be very depressing when you have a job that isn't right for you."

Readers arrive at conclusions by making connections from their own experiences and formulate solutions by listening to the events in the lives of other readers. The written entry of the Lit Log expands into the great conversations of the lit group as students negotiate meaning.

Negotiating Meaning

As readers mature in this ability to negotiate meaning with other group members, they begin to listen to other ideas and alter or change their own. After hearing alternative ideas, conclusions, or solutions, children modify their original thoughts to include a new twist in their thinking. They quickly learn that there are multiple perspectives to choose from when contemplating a solution. The following is a dialogue from a discussion of *On the Far Side of the Mountain*:

Natalie: How do you feel about this? Alice and Crystal left many signs like tracks and scrambled leaves. Bando and Sam set out to find Alice. They used maps and signs to

track her. They are getting closer to her.

Val: I think Alice is just playing a game and that they should go back and wait for her at home.

Ryan: Well, I wonder if she is hiding out or that guy is dragging her or if she just ran away by herself.

Natalie: Oh, and maybe she left that note to, you know, fool Sam, or that person made her do it. I don't know.

Val: Well, if she has been taken then I think they are getting closer to her every day, and they shouldn't worry so much.

Natalie: Plus pigs have a vicious bite it said in the book. This would be good for protection. It also said pigs were very intelligent.

Ryan: It seems like Alice planned her trip well.

Val: Maybe too well!

Natalie initiated the conversation by stating several facts that the whole group knew from the reading. She drew others into the conversation by asking, "How do you feel about this?" There were several different views of the situation. Val had one view at the beginning of the conversation. Ryan created the possibility of three different explanations for Alice's disappearance. After Ryan revealed his thoughts, Natalie made a connection between his idea about being kidnapped and the note. From Natalie's connection, Val, who at the beginning of the discussion thought the search for Alice was a waste of time, speculates on the idea that maybe someone snatched her. Natalie continues to share more information from the book, which once again sparks a new idea from Ryan. Val then adds a little suspicion to the conversation by implying that all the events seem too perfect.

As the group built their dialogue, it was obvious how meaning was negotiated from reader to reader. It reminded me of a snowball rolling downhill, collecting snow and getting larger. The collaborative ideas grew into a continuous dialogue. It is essential that the members of the group become good listeners. The ability to listen to others and create new ideas deepens the quality of the dialogue.

How Literature Groups Evolve Over Time

Great literature groups aren't built in a day. I've found that they develop along the following timetable:

First Month

The children are shy and some are reluctant to read their logs aloud. Some speak very quietly, others read from their Lit Logs closely, and have little to add.

Second Month

Most children are becoming excited about reading their logs and begin to make comments in discussion that they haven't already written down. Even the reluctant ones begin to read their logs aloud.

Third Month

The children are often scrambling for a turn at sharing. They become more critical listeners. They begin to analyze the characters and events more closely.

Fourth Month

The children are almost competing on an intellectual level. Not in a rude or obnoxious manner, but with a feeling or need to find or uncover ideas that are unique to the group.

Fifth Month

The children hone their literary skills and begin to stretch their thinking to a higher level. This continues to grow for the rest of the year.

Debate

As this behavior continues to grow into intriguing and challenging dialogue within the group, a new aspect of group discussion appears. Dialogue naturally turns into a debate when the text presents two sides of a powerful issue. Children feel safe enough to debate an issue with all the members of the group when a secure environment exists. Children debate with each other only when they feel their opinions will be respected during and after the study group time. When children feel strongly about an idea, they substantiate their stand on the issue with little flexibility.

One of the most memorable debates took place in a literature circle without my participation. Students gathered at the literature table, and the debate began. I was on the outside of the circle, listening. *Freedom Crossing* was the literature being debated.

Student 1: I'm really angry at Laura for not wanting to help the slave escape.
Student 2: I'm not. It was her brother who was doing the wrong thing.
Student 3: What was Bert doing wrong?
Student 2: He was helping a slave run away.
Student 1: How could you stand by and not help the slaves?
Student 2: Oh, I really felt sorry for them, but it was against the law to help slaves run away. My mom says we should never break the law.
Student 1: I know it was against the law, but it was a very bad law. We should always help people in need.
Student 3: You both have a good point. I think the way to solve this problem would be to help change the bad law on slavery. If we don't like a law, there are ways that we can change it.

Student 1 and Student 2 had definite opinions about a very controversial issue. Neither student was willing to compromise their position on the matter. Student 3 acted as a mediator on the issue by pointing out a solution that would satisfy both sides without threatening their beliefs. Students showed respect for each other's opinion and calmly presented each side of the issue. The ability to debate a point of view within the realm of a literature group demonstrates a desirable level of real dialogue.

Playing the Role of the Facilitator in Literature Groups

As teachers we play many roles. When you teach with literature circles, one role you'll assume is that of facilitator. It is a multi-faceted role. The teacher's goal is to evoke responses or conversation, not guide or direct them. Too much interference results in a teacher-centered exchange of ideas. Teacher-centered dialogues inhibit a child's response to the literature. Teachers must seek out the "focus moments" that arise in the group conversation. Those "moments" allow the teacher to focus on ideas charged with meaning. The teacher heightens the group's comprehension by identifying and naming literary elements as they arise in the discussion (Peterson and Eeds, 1990).

❦

Literary Elements for Focus

The following is a list of literary elements that will bring focus to almost any Literature Study Group discussion. Students might not know what to call the element they are describing, so the teacher can give it a label. This list can also be used by teachers to enhance their own Lit Log entries and for mini-lessons.

- Story Setting
- Character Analysis
- Discovering the Plot
- Narrator
- Mood
- Figurative Language
- Drawing Conclusions
- Illustrations
- Relating Personally
- Comparison/Contrast
- Developing Generalizations
- Author's Purpose
- Analyzing Problems/Formulating Solutions
- Creating New Ideas
- Critiquing the Author's Style
- Author's Purpose
- Evaluating with Reasons

The goal of teachers is to facilitate the dialogue by initiating and maintaining literature discussions to help the students explore the text in depth. A few guidelines will help clarify the teacher's role as a member of the literature circle.

- Support the conversation, don't dominate it.
- Encourage students to explore new possibilities; don't advocate only recall of facts.
- Engage the conversation through the children's understanding; don't impose adult meanings.

- Share your own literacy by demonstrating how you read, write, and respond to literature.
- Provide support for students' story ideas.
- Foster good peer listening practices; don't reiterate and reword students' responses.
- Assist children in becoming independent; don't create dependence as the group leader.
- Follow the flow of conversation; don't try to constantly redirect the discussion.

The teacher's responsibility is to aid in the growth of the community's social behavior. Simple rules of courtesy bring order to the discussion group. Students use the literature circle time more productively when they practice what I call "quality sharing practices."

❦

Management Tips for Quality Sharing Practices

For all this learning to take place, some guidelines for group behavior must be set and reinforced. This list of tips was brainstormed by the students and teacher in a whole-group session, but it is reviewed during individual study group sessions as a reminder. I share positive comments when I see what I call "quality behavior" taking place (some teachers call this "catching them being good.") For example, "Carianne, I loved the way you paid close attention while Levi was speaking." This encourages others to behave in like manner.

- Give eye contact to the speaker.
- Speak only an appropriate amount of time.
- Take turns speaking.
- Listen to the discussion.
- Share your thoughts in an appropriate manner.

If group members follow these suggestions, the group focus will be strictly on the literature.

Reflections

From my experience in the classroom, I've discovered that children do not engage in ideal discussion sessions immediately. That does not mean that group meetings are a waste of time until the children begin to engage in real dialogue. Many early sessions will consist of each child clinging to the words of the Lit Log and adding nothing more to the conversation. This is part of feeling safe while sharing ideas with classmates. The teacher is the heart of the community. I begin by establishing links between the members, so children can begin to make group connections on their own. We must be patient with the children's progress and view each discussion as a growing, bonding community experience. As facilitators of the literature circle, we must guide the focus of the discussion toward a meaningful learning experience. We must control the urge to govern the group. The success of a focused discussion group centers around an atmosphere created through the mutual trust of students and teacher. I find myself anticipating daily literature study circles with great excitement. It is so exhilarating to be part of this learning process. Every day the readers take new steps toward creating meaning from literature, and I am there to view that magnificent occurrence in the lives of my students.

— Penny

Chapter 8

Literature Extensions and Responses

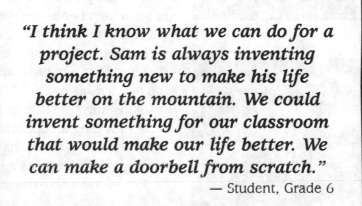

"I think I know what we can do for a project. Sam is always inventing something new to make his life better on the mountain. We could invent something for our classroom that would make our life better. We can make a doorbell from scratch."

— Student, Grade 6

Literature Extensions and Responses in Context

Good literature naturally empowers the reader to respond in a variety of ways. After reading *Dear Mr. Henshaw*, many readers feel compelled to begin their own personal diary in addition to their Lit Logs. The book *Tuck Everlasting* might spring to mind whenever they encounter the life cycle in other literary works or in real life experiences. These examples point out two different types of literature extensions or responses. The diary demonstrates a hands-on participatory change and *Tuck Everlasting* evokes a change in thoughts. One is extrinsic, and the other is intrinsic.

Purpose

The purpose for literature extensions is to stretch and enhance the students' experiences of the text, directly encouraging the reading/writing connections. Literature extensions should reflect a natural desire to continue where the text left off by:

- Inspiring ideas to enhance the literature
- Providing an opportunity for readers to express connections they made
- Allowing students to spend meaningful time revisiting the story.

Literature extension activities can be presented in many styles:

- Board Games
- Panel Discussions
- Newscast Reports
- Drama (Plays)
- Courtroom Trial
- Creating Mobiles

- Creating Murals
- Writing and Illustrating Cartoons and Comic Strips.

These type of extensions tap into children's diverse intelligences, allowing them many opportunities to express their strengths through art, music, or writing in a variety of formats, such as acting, problem solving, and so on.

Some organizational reminders I've found helpful in preparing groups for their presentations:

- A monthly calendar of events and due dates
- Daily reminders for each group on the class schedule

- Meetings with group leaders for daily updates
- Scheduled 'preview' conferences to check for group readiness

Getting Started with Extension Activities

Many extensions apply to any work of literature. They are general means of extending the literature to bring greater understanding of the story. Examples of extension activities follow.

Story Mapping

Children reconstruct the literature by mapping out the structure and literary elements of the story. See the samples below and on the next page.

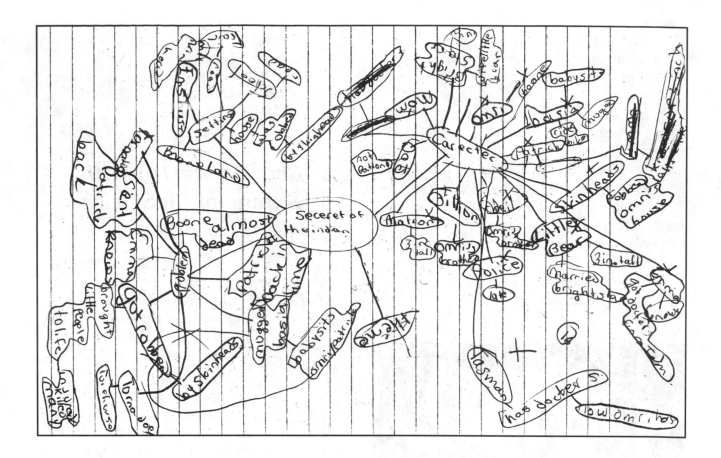

Venn Diagram

Readers can show comparisons and contrasts between characters, settings, moods, plots, etc., as seen below.

Writing a Play

The students gain experience as playwrights by revisiting the literature and changing its form. The use of the computer makes editing and formatting easy. See samples on page 69.

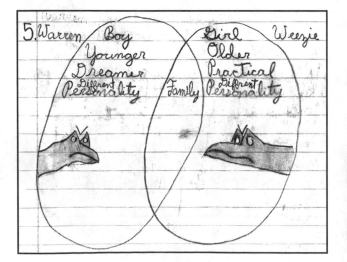

"Nighty Nightmare"

Narrator: Chester, Harold, Howie, and the Monroes all went on a camping trip. They kept walking and walking in the woods. First they saw two men and a dog that scared them. Then they saw something else. And in this chapter, it will tell what they saw.

Harold : My legs ache from walking.

Dawg: Come on, follow me. Ain't it a sight! Come on let's go closer.

Harold: I'm too scared to go any farther.

Chester: I think maybe we should go back to camp. Do you know the way, Dawg?

Dawg: Ah come on. Don't start that chicken stuff again .

Harold: Don't you want to get back to the camp?

Dawg: Well sure, but don't you wanna see the house?

Howie: I want to go home.

Dawg: We've come all this way. You want to see it don't you Howie?

Howie: I don't want to go to that house! I'll go anywhere but that house. Let's go back to camp!

Chester: We don't have much time until midnight. And the last thing we want to do is go in that house.

Dawg: Well, O.K. (yawning)

Narrator: They saw a spooky old house that looked like a cathedral to them. This is a spooky and exciting book. We liked it, and we hope you will too.

"Jim Ugly"

Story Teller: Once upon a time lived a boy named Jake. He is trying to find his dad. Jake has a dog named Jim Ugly.

Jake: I'm setting out to find my dad.

Willi: But it's soaking wet out there.

Jake: But I want to find my dad.

Willi: But it's still wet, you're going to catch a cold.

Story Teller: Jake went out to find his dad. And the yellow leg was following him.

Yellow Leg: Who are you?

Jake: I'm Jake.

Yellow Leg: What are you doing?

Jake: I'm trying to find my dad.

Yellow Leg: Who is your dad?

Jake: I don't know.

Yellow Leg: How are you trying to find your dad?

Jake: I don't know.

Story Teller: He went to Sunflower Creek and found Willi there.

Willi: Would you like to be in the play?

Jake: Yes I would.

Story Teller: The night of the play Jake's dad walked up behind him.

Jake: Dad!

Story Teller: But Jake's dad didn't hear him.

Composing Music

Children love music! Story when set to music provides a natural reaction to the literature. The children can use a variety of musical instruments to compose a piece of music. The members of a literature circle created the song below as a group. One student brought a keyboard to school. The group as a whole worked diligently in the hall just outside the classroom trying different melodies to fit the lyrics, and involving the music teacher when they were ready to put the notes on paper.

Additional General Ways of Extending Literature

- *Research projects*
- *Interviewing experts*
- *Poetry, essay, story, journal*
- *Artistic creations (posters, sculptures, etc.)*
- *Class newsletter*
- *Cooking*
- *Drama (e.g. reenacting scenes)*

Specific Extension Ideas

Other extensions may be tailor-made for a particular piece of literature. After reading a book about a summer camp, students decided to create brochures for their own camps. The group members embraced the idea of researching advertising techniques. Each student individually created a brochure highlighting the different attractions of the camp (see samples on page 72). One group member brought back several brochures from the local tourist center for the group to look at. The group decided to make their brochures tri-fold in form. On each flap of the tri-fold, they placed information uniquely descriptive of their camps. The finished product was eye-catching, colorful, and creative. The group then created a ballot sheet containing each of the camp names. Together the group visited every classroom in the building. They

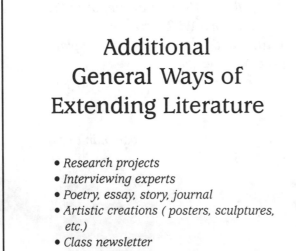

took turns presenting their brochures, outlining the benefits of their camps. After the group completed the presentations, they handed out ballots to each child in the different classrooms. The children who voted marked their ballots, which were collected and taken to the literature group's classroom. The lit group counted ballots and recorded the outcome. They created a huge wall chart and posted it in the hall for all the students to view. (I personally voted for Camp Clean, but, surprisingly enough, it placed last.)

Jelly Belly

The book *Jelly Belly* created a great awareness of proper eating habits. The Literature Study Group decided to monitor their own junk food intake for a week. They created recording charts for each member and spent a week recording all the junk food they consumed. When the week was over, they each designed a pictograph of the results. They carefully studied their own graphs to determine on which days they consumed the most junk food. This led to a valuable discussion as they shared thoughts about why they ate more junk food on certain days of the week. These personal discoveries helped each group member become aware of undesirable eating habits.

Jelly Belly's Junk Food Chart		in all 3,376
Sat.	Chips 345	345
Sun.	Dad's cake 130, Soda 145, Doritos 345	620
Mon.	Hot Dog 291, Chips 345, Fudge	636
Tues.	Fudge 145	145
Wed.	Rolo 115, Chocolate candy 145, Waffle 210	470
Thurs.	candy 115, mints, pizza 425, chips 345	915
Fri.	Donuts 150, candy, mints 145	295

I'm a Junk food ... Chart Jelly Belly — Total amount of calories in a week 3,576

Sat.		345 calories in chips
Sun		620 calories in Dad's cake, Soda, and Doritos
Mon.		636 calories in Hot dog, chips, and Fudge
Tues.		145 calories in Fudge
Wed.		470 calories in Rolo, Chocolate candy, and a Waffle
Thurs.		915 calories in candy mints, pizza, and chips
Fri.		245 calories in Donuts, and candy mints

Sideways Stories

Many children enjoy reading *Sideways Stories from Wayside School* by Louis Sachar. One of the most exciting projects to come from this text was a simple piggyback book. The group decided to interview every student in the classroom to find out their personality traits. The group then began to create a book about our classroom that resembled the classroom in Sachar's book. It turned out to be a delightfully written representation of classroom personalities. The class thought it was so good that they published it and sold copies before school outside the classroom for an entire week. The demand was so great that the group had to print additional copies. It was a humorous extension project that turned into a literary success, and the entire school body thoroughly enjoyed it.

Literature extensions can be accomplished by an individual, a pair, several members of the group, or the whole group. The children should choose the type of extension and develop a plan for its completion. Literature extensions chosen by the teacher will not be productive and will stifle the creativity of the group. Making the presentation gives purpose to the literature extension.

Teachers can help each group organize and create the product they have in mind. Teachers are an important part of the group. We can be actively engaged in the extension activities in any of the following ways. We can:

- Share ideas used by other students that created similar extension projects.
- Encourage the group to assign each member a job to organize the activity.
- Provide creative ideas that will enhance the activity.

- Work closely with the members by being available to organize materials.

Camp Brochures

The stories within the covers of this book are about the students of Room 108. These children attend a school in Hannibal, MO called Oakwood Elementary. Oakwood is the tallest school in the city. The men, who were building it, made a very large error. They thought they were building a skyscraper and they built the classrooms straight up.

Even though this caused a lot of problems, there was an extremely large playground around the school.

Some people, who know the students, think that these stories are definitely true. You will have to decide for yourself.

Mrs. Strube is tall, thin and wears holsters with disinfectant spray guns. She detests germs. Every day she sprays and cleans room 108 until it sparkles. All of her students must have their temperature taken before Mrs. Strube allows them to breathe in the room. If a student has a sibling that is ill, she makes her student stay at school all night so they don't go home and breathe the same germy air. The children all wear plastic bags over their shoes and remove them when they enter the room. That way the floor stays spotless. There are boxes of Kleenex on each desk accompanied by a small box of wet ones. There are colored drop cloths to cover all of the room during an art project. Every morning, Mrs. Strube has the children chant the room motto: "A room that is clean, Is a good learning scene."

In education today, there is a growing desire to break away from superficial extension activities and move toward more thoughtful literature enhancements. Many of my

literature groups do not develop a desire to get involved in an extension activity. I do not insist, strongly encourage, or pressure students into project involvement. If the group decides the story needs an extension, I assist and guide them toward a meaningful activity.

After reading one particular work of literature, one group decided to make a gameboard using as many of the story elements as possible. I remember thinking to myself, "What a waste of time," but the whole group was so enthusiastic about the project, that I kept my thoughts to myself. The group worked together exceptionally well as they planned and designed the playing board. I periodically eavesdropped on the group's conversations as they worked. The students reentered the text constantly to create the perfect character game pieces. Students drew each character to match the author's exact description. The setting was duplicated on the game board. The key item in the book was a locket. One of the girls brought a locket from home and placed it in the middle of the board as the prize for the winner of the game. In the book the characters faced many problems that were placed on the game board as setbacks. The game squares progressed in perfect sequence with the plot of the story. Each member referred constantly to the text to ensure an accurate interpretation of the author's work. The process, as well as the end result, completely amazed me. Every student in the room wanted to play the game. The group presented the game board to the entire class and stored it in the rainy-day game drawer. What I thought would be a total waste of time turned out to be a precise piece of collaborative work. I love it when children show me the way!

— Penny

Chapter 9

Strategies for Further Interaction with Text

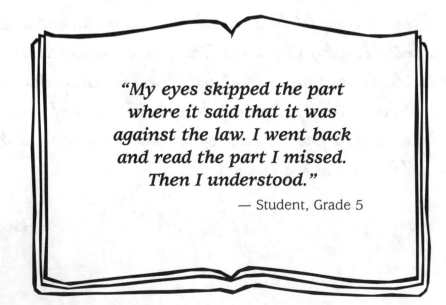

"My eyes skipped the part where it said that it was against the law. I went back and read the part I missed. Then I understood."

— Student, Grade 5

Two Types of Strategies

The term *reading strategies* usually refers to strategies used to make sense of print (comprehension), not to strategies that enhance an understanding of the literary elements. To create independent readers, teachers help students use strategies to make sense of the text. To encourage readers to become meaning makers, teachers provide strategies that investigate literary elements. Both types of strategies are important if readers are to find success in their literature studies, but the latter strategy is the one I'll focus on here. The following strategies are ones that I have found successful in helping my students recognize and discuss literary elements.

A Word on Fix-Up Strategies for Attending to Print

When children read and come to an unfamiliar word, fix-up strategies serve as a guide in solving their reading dilemma. The fix-up strategies require the learner to read on and confirm that the strategy produced a result that makes sense. Common fix-up strategies include:

- Substitute another word.
- Reread the passage to see if any part was inadvertently missed or read incorrectly.
- Skip it and use the context of the following sentences to gather additional meaning.
- Use the illustrations to create mental pictures to gain insight for substituting.
- Sound it out (use sound/symbol relationship).
- Seek out a peer to help.
- Use paired reading to maintain a support system for the readers.

Strategies for Understanding Literary Elements

Strategies that create a literacy environment are used before, during, and after the children read and discuss literature. I teach the following strategies for understanding literary elements as it seems appropriate to whole class or small groups. The strategies themselves are used as the students find the need, at any time while reading or discussing the literature.

One strategy may be versatile enough to explicate greater meaning for a variety of literature elements. Using the elements outlined by Peterson and Eeds (*Grand Conversations*, Scholastic, 1990)– structure, plot, character and tension– the following commonly used strategies will elevate the student's ability to interpret the text.

NOTE: Full-size reproducible copies of the charts and worksheets can be found in the Appendix. Copy and keep on hand for students to use as needed.

Literary Element: Structure

The structure of the story includes the sequence from beginning to end. It also gives a designed framework that holds the story elements together. I model the following strategies by filling in and discussing story maps and grids with the group as we discuss a piece of literature.

- **Story Maps**— Story maps provide a visual image of the story structure while giving names to the elements. See sample on page 79.
- **Story Grids**— Story grids allow the student to put the story in sequence by filling each square with an event. They provide another visual look at the story as the events unfold. A story grid is a type of story time line. See sample on page 80.

Literary Element: Plot

The plot is an easily identifiable literary element. Children quickly relate one event to another and the way in which the events build on each other. See sample on page 81.

Literary Element: Character

The characters in a story all play an important role. The size of the role may vary, but it does not diminish the character's importance. Main characters usually get the most focus from the story. Their roles develop and they experience some form of transformation.

- **Character Maps**— Character maps provide visual images of the characters and their personalities, attributes, and so on. Children create their own kinds of character maps. Both the generic form and the creative form create a visual interpretation of the characters. See samples on pages 82 and 83.
- **Character Analysis Webs**— Using the familiar technique of webbing, readers can create a visual representation of the connections among characters as they are woven together in the story. Readers can analyze each character's personality and

determine the relationships to other characters. The character being analyzed or explored would be in the center of the web, creating an entanglement of associations that surround it.

- **Venn Diagrams**— Another way of examining the characters in a story is by using the Venn diagram. This is the perfect tool for comparisons and contrasts. Although this strategy applies to almost all of the literature elements, pointing out how two characters have completely different personalities and yet still have something in common leads to a better understanding of character diversity. See sample on page 84.

Literary Element: Tension

The story's tension is the engine that propels the reader's desire to become engrossed in the literature. Tension causes the reader to feel the emotion of the events as they occur as well as of events to follow. Prediction strategies encourage readers to free their imaginations and explore endless twists and turns the story could take in its journey toward a conclusion.

- **Tension Graphs**— A tension graph is a continuous line that shows how the tension builds and falls throughout the story.
- **Prediction Charts**— Readers use prediction charts to record their predictions before reading a passage and also to confirm the actual events that occurred. A prediction chart therefore becomes a before-reading and after-reading chart. Some charts include the reader's thoughts and interpretation of the clues given in the text. See samples on pages 85 and 86.
- **Clues from the Cover**— This is a prereading, prediction strategy. Clues from the cover encourage readers to engage their imaginations and use their prior knowledge to make predictions about a book before they open it. The clues may emanate from

Sample Story Map

Title/Author: "Tuck Everlasting" by Natalie Babbit

Setting: A village called Treegap in the 1880's

Main Characters: Winnie, Mae, Tuck, Jesse and Miles

Problem: Winnie discovers the spring.

Events: Winnie is kidnapped as she is trying to drink from the spring. The Tuck family is living forever. The Tucks and Winnie become good friends. Tuck tries to explain the circle of life to Winnie.

Solutions: Winnie must decide what to do in her own life. She chooses to live a normal life instead of never dying.

Story Theme: Life is a wheel. All things in life travel in a circle or a cycle for a reason.

Sample Story Grid

Title/ Author: "The Secret of the Seal"

by Deborah Davis

1. Kyo's uncle came and everyone was happy.	2. His uncle began talking about zoos.	3. He drew pictures of the animals and told all about them.	4. Suddenly he mentions that he needs a seal..
5. Kyo tries to convince him that it is not a good day for hunting.	6. Kyo orders Tooky the seal back to the sea before he is seen.	7. Kyo, his father and his uncle go seal hunting.	8. Kyo is so very afraid.
9. They don't catch any seals.	10. Kyo misses Tooky.	11. Kyo can't sleep and goes to Tooky's ice hole.	12. The ice hole is closed up.
13. Uncle George breaks the ice on Tooky's hole.	14. The seal's head pops up and Uncle George kills her.	15. Kyo is very angry.	16. Kyo runs away.

Sample Plot Chart
(Cause & Effect)

Title/Author: "Traitor" by Jean Fritz

Event Happened	Event Caused	Resulting Effect
Joshua Smith is serving.	Joshua Smith saw Livingston in a British uniform.	He had second thoughts about keeping his job.
Major Andre is traveling with papers.	Major Andre was caught.	He became a prisoner of war and was hanged.
Patriots suspect Benedict Arnold.	Arnold was exposed as a traitor.	Arnold has to try to explain his reasons for being a traitor.

Sample Character Map

Title/Author: "Freedom Crossing"
                  by Margaret Goff Clark

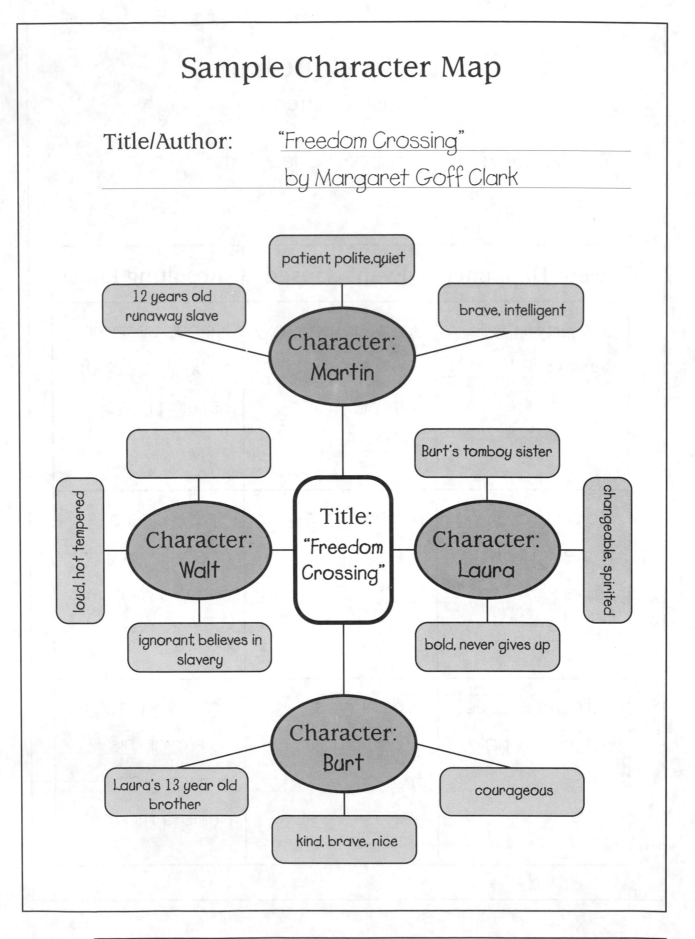

patient, polite, quiet

12 years old runaway slave

brave, intelligent

Character: Martin

Burt's tomboy sister

loud, hot tempered

Character: Walt

Title: "Freedom Crossing"

Character: Laura

changeable, spirited

ignorant, believes in slavery

bold, never gives up

Character: Burt

Laura's 13 year old brother

courageous

kind, brave, nice

knowledge of the author or illustrator, and from the title, cover art, or descriptive blurb on the back. The following is a sample of a child's response to the clues from the cover strategy:

"I looked at the back of the cover of *Jim Ugly* by Sid Fleischman. I think Jake's father is not dead. His father is probably hiding somewhere. I know this book is funny because Sid Fleischman wrote *Whipping Boy*. I read that book and it was funny. It looks to me like Jim Ugly is Jake's best friend right now. The setting could be somewhere far away from us, because the land looks different."

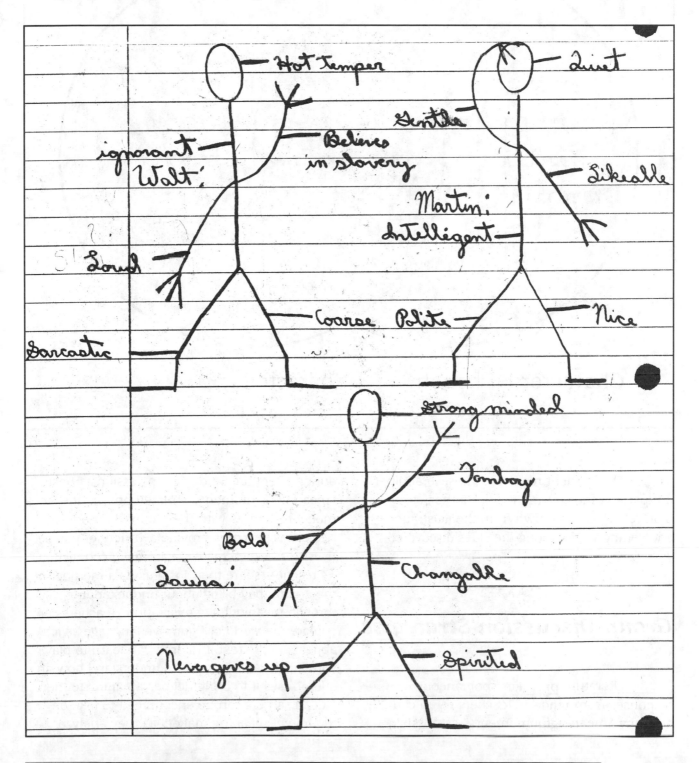

Sample Venn Diagram

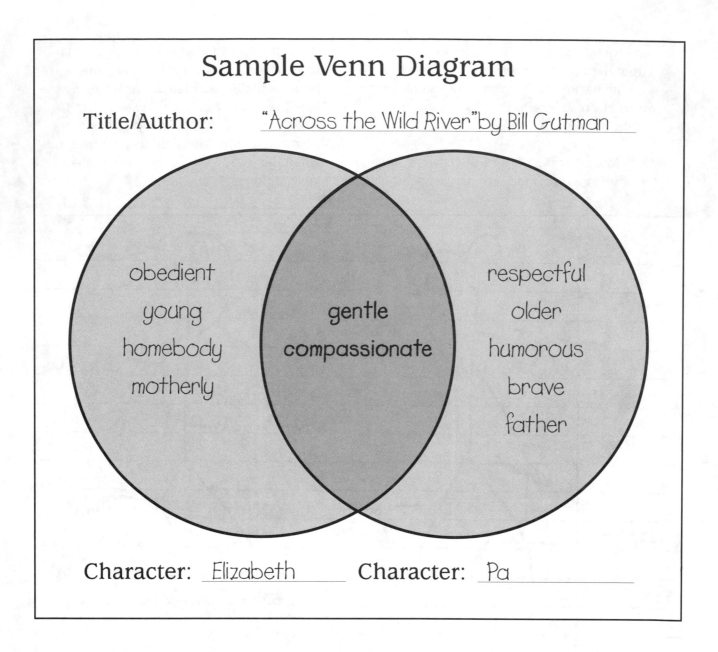

Title/Author: "Across the Wild River" by Bill Gutman

obedient
young
homebody
motherly

gentle
compassionate

respectful
older
humorous
brave
father

Character: Elizabeth   Character: Pa

This student responded to several different parts of the cover. The title, author, story plot, relationships drawn from the illustration, and setting were among the clues discovered.

⁓✖⁓

Group Discussion Strategies

Literature provokes spontaneous responses from readers. Teachers try to capture as many "meaningful moments" as possible during Literature Study Group sessions. Those "meaningful moments" create opportunities to model responses with the group. By modeling responses, teachers provide a variety of perspectives from which readers can make connections. As teachers share their insights as a member of the group, they bring about understanding through meaningful conversation. Teachers can explore the world of figurative language as it appears in the text. Children can learn to play with language and begin to understand how an author uses it to bring deeper meaning to the story. Learners can be encouraged to take on the role of meaning makers as they analyze

Sample Prediction Chart #1

Title/Author: "Across the Wild River" by Bill Gutman

Clues from the Text	Your Interpretation	Your Prediction
Jeremy came back for his family. He said his place was with his family.	It sounds like he has grown up a little.	I think he will stay with them this time.
The storm was terrible. The sound was so loud and the wind was wild.	The storm was severe like the storms we have in the summer.	After the storm, someone will catch a chill and become very sick.
The colt was bony. It had knobby knees, bony hips and a shaggy coat.	I guess he wasn't cared for by Mr. Meacham properly.	I believe with a lot of care the colt will grow to be a worthy horse.

Sample Prediction Chart #2

Title/Author: "Freedom Crossing"
                  by Margaret Goff Clark

Prediction Before Reading	Actual Happening
Martin is a slave. He is uneducated and won't be able to do the same things that Burt and Laura can do.	Martin could read, write and even spell. His "Pappy" taught him.
The slave catchers will come to the house, but they won't come in.	The slave catchers do come to the house, and they do come in to look for Martin.
They will try to hide Martin in the cellar.	They hide Martin in the secret room instead of the cellar.

problems confronting the characters and their situations. Children become confident meaning makers as they analyze problems, formulate solutions, evaluate characters and situations, and create new ideas.

Literature Response Strategies

Some strategies that support the interpretations created during Literature Study Groups can be found in *Creating Classrooms for Authors* by Jerome Harste, Kathy Short, and Carolyn Burke (Heineman, 1988). You can teach the strategies when you work with groups on an "as needed" basis and/or assign them as you judge students to be ready for them. These teacher-proven strategies always generate student interaction and result in deeper thinking. These activities can be done **before, during,** or **after** class literature group meeting time, and presented during group discussion or other class time.

Webbing

This strategy is so motivating! During group discussion time, as students contribute their thoughts to the group, questions and issues sparked by the literature arise. These can be written by you or a student as a web on the chalkboard or a chart. Additional discussion develops as the readers move around the web, bringing deeper meaning to the story.

"Sketch to Stretch"

This strategy creates a trusting atmosphere among readers. Students sketch a meaningful scene from the story or simply relate through a rough sketch the meaning they gathered from the story. One student exhibits the

sketch to the rest of the group. All students in the Literature Study Group express their thoughts and interpretations about their peer's sketch. The student artist reveals the original thoughts behind the sketch. The group then discusses the diverse ideas brought about by each sketch.

Pondering Quotes or Passages

As students read, they come to passages or quotes that need their further consideration. Before group time, the student as he reads, jots down the passage for sharing with the group when they meet. The group then tosses around different thoughts and explanations about the passage.

Free Writing

When the entire literature group finishes reading a book, a certain amount of time is allotted for the students to write during part of their group discussion time. They write freely about anything related to the literature. They continue to write until time is up. Students read all or part of their writing to the group and discussion revolves around the responses. When students exhaust their thoughts on one free writing sample, they move on to another student's writing until the entire group has had the opportunity to share.

Word Wall

Before group discussion time begins, students gather around a large sheet of paper fixed to the wall and write on it words or phases connected with the story. Each student creates a visual word collage on the paper. The group creation then becomes a focal point for discussion during the rest of the group time. As new ideas form, they are added to the word wall.

Book Logs

To integrate content knowledge with literature, students keep a group log in addition to their individual Lit Logs. The log is organized around the brainstorming format of "What I know," "What I want to know," and "What I've learned." During group discussion time, the group collectively records all prior knowledge on the subject or theme of the book. Members record what questions they have about the subject prior to reading. When an answer surfaces in the text, the students record it in the log. The log becomes an ongoing record of the process of interweaving prior knowledge with new knowledge.

Studying Stance

Stance is an attitude or position taken about a certain subject. By assuming different stances as they write in their Lit Logs before discussion time, students can look at a piece of literature through different perspectives. This allows them to feel and make meaning with a new outlook. When looking at literature from a writer's stance, readers perceive literature through style, voice, and cadence. They look at how the author shares and creates the story. When taking a reader's stance, students mentally visualize how characters cope throughout the book. They examine tension and how characters deal with it. Children might look for symbolism and attempt to unravel its meaning as it applies to the story.

Reflections

Each year before school begins, I contemplate a variety of ways to create a "love of literature" in the hearts of my new students. Last year out of our desperate need for money to feed our collection of fish and hermit crabs, I suggested that my class start a book business. The children and I brainstormed how our business would function as part of our daily routine. Students formed committees to discuss all the aspects of starting a business.

The needs list was not long, but going into business together would require some sacrifice of personal time, talent, and property. The first order of business was to choose a suitable name. Students wrote their favorite name on a sheet of paper. I transferred the suggestions to an overhead transparency. They took a vote and chose the name "Book Nook." The group decided that each student in the room should be responsible for some part of the business. The job committee posted the jobs, and the interviewing process began. The job committee created enough positions to accommodate every student in the room.

There were five departments needed to successfully run the "Book Nook." The departments were purchasing (book buyers), finance (banker, bookkeepers), advertising, sales (book sellers), and pricing (sorters, price markers). The children wrote resumés and all received jobs in the business. To get started, each student brought three paperbacks from home and donated them to the "Book Nook."

As the year progressed, I was astonished by the knowledge and excitement that was being expressed about books. The whole room became a business community. The book buyers were purchasing only books with good reading value. In their own words, "Boring books won't sell." The advertising committee had an excellent campaign of signs, posters, and morning announcements spoken over the intercom. They created jingles that caught on around the school. "Get hooked on books at the Book Nook," was their favorite. The children worked together to build a productive business, and they were extremely successful. But the most exciting aspect of the business venture proved to be the way the students became so involved with literature. They valued the literature, and its influence permeated their daily conversations. They had acquired the "love of literature" as I had hoped at the beginning of our business adventure.

— Penny

THE BOOK NOOK!

THE BOOK NOOK SELLS LAMINATED BOOK MARKS NOW!HURRY UP AND BUY YOUR BOOK MARKS TODAY,WHILE SUPPLIES LAST!

THERE'S ANOTHER THING NEW.SOON WE'LL HAVE PAPER,TOO.(MADE BY US)

      Sincerely,
THE BOOK NOOK

Chapter 10

Assessment
and
Evaluation

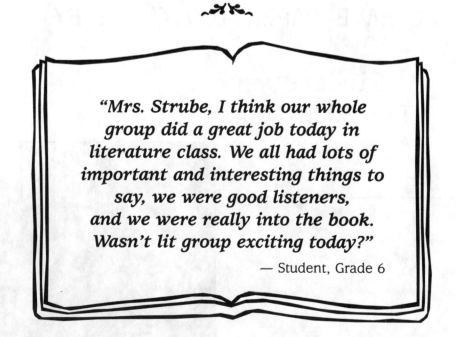

*"Mrs. Strube, I think our whole
group did a great job today in
literature class. We all had lots of
important and interesting things to
say, we were good listeners,
and we were really into the book.
Wasn't lit group exciting today?"*

— Student, Grade 6

Evaluation— Not Just for Teachers

The ability to assess and evaluate experiences comes naturally to children. They often know instinctively if something is good or bad, and usually they can explain how to improve it. But formal assessment and evaluation are not always simple for teachers. It can be difficult to explain the difference between assessment and evaluation, because they are interwoven. The two intertwine and complement each other. Assessment is the foundation of evaluation.

When assessing, the teacher gathers information and confirmation of her ideas about a student's reading abilities. When evaluating, the teacher attaches value or significance to the information after carefully analyzing it.

Evaluation in Literature Studies

Dorothy Watson, my professor at the University of Missouri, describes authentic evaluation for literature study in these terms (*Talking About Books*, Heinemann, 1990):

- **Not Competitive—** Students rarely ask about their grades. They self-evaluate and make adjustments instinctively. Therefore, they are always trying to improve themselves. They do not compete against other readers. While striving to improve themselves, they try to help others as well. It is not a race to make a grade. It is a journey to become the best each can be while helping others along the way.

- **Internally Motivating—** When teachers help children understand that evaluation is internally motivating, students strive to become more proficient readers. They desire to quench an internal desire to reach their potential.
- **Perpetual—** Evaluation is not a sporadic process. It is continuous. To arrive at a true picture of a child's growth, teachers must evaluate at all times.
- **Informative—** Evaluation provides needed information for children and all those involved with their learning. Evaluation informs teachers and allows them to adjust strategies to increase learning.

Benchmarks for Evaluation

I believe that literature study yields proficient readers who:
- Construct meaning
- Apply fix-up strategies such as:
  - sound it out
  - use sentence structure
  - substitute
  - skip it and keep on going to gather inferences
  - use picture clues
  - know where to get help
- Self-correct
- Connect knowledge
- Enjoy reading
- Read critically
- Take risks

I evaluate my students based on these benchmarks of proficiency to monitor their progress from beginning readers to masterful readers.

The Evaluation Process

Reading evaluation may take place before, during, and after reading. There is no set time or activity for the evaluation process. Every time a child has a book in hand or is engaged in gaining meaning from print, an evaluation opportunity presents itself in the form of "data" to be "collected" by the observant teacher. This data collection takes place through performance sampling, observations, and conversations.

Performance Samplings

The students allow an observer to enter their world of reading by sharing the reading process in an oral or written form.

- **Tape Recording—** Before, during and after children read a book, they record a short piece from the story on their own cassette tape. The tape becomes a continuous record of their oral reading throughout the year.
- **Oral Reading—** Children read to each other, to teachers, or to a group. Oral reading takes place in a reader's theater setting or in the corner of the room.
- **Literature Logs—** Book responses written as literature logs provide a sample of the reader's written expression. Because students respond in various ways in a literature log, the log provides samples of different kinds of writing.

Observations

In both quiet and active times, the teacher can easily collect abundant information through simple observations. Yetta Goodman calls this "Kidwatching." Observation is an important element in the data collection process.

An observer learns so much by watching the reader as he or she reads in authentic situations.

- **Independent Reading—** The independent reader provides valuable information through silent movements, such as mannerisms. The reader's choice of book, way of holding a book, attention given to print, and time spent with a book, convey important information regarding level of interest, degree of difficulty or ease, etc.
- **Discussion—** As the readers reveal their thoughts and ideas through literature-group dialogue, they display many observable traits. They show growth as they gain new thoughts from the discussion of others. They disclose how the story elements work for them as a reader. Listening to their discussions will allow you to add your informal observations.

Conversations

Having conversations, or one-on-one interviews with students is a very comfortable way of collecting information.

- **Formal Conversations—** A formal conversation is an interview that is prepared

Sample Questions:

- *Which character was your favorite? Why?*
- *Which character were you not fond of? Why?*
- *When did the story seem to have tension?*
- *Were there some weak parts in the story? How would you have changed the story to correct the weak areas?*
- *Did you enjoy the book? Why or why not?*

ahead of time. Teachers have the opportunity to set up a battery of questions that they believe will enable them to help the reader to improve. *The Burke Reading Interview* (Goodman, Watson, Burke, 1987) is a formal individual interview that draws on general questions that allow the teacher to examine how the student views reading. A formal interview about a specific work of literature often brings insight to both teacher and student. General questions provide a format adaptable to any literary work.

- **Informal Conversations—** Informal conversations are not prepared or prescribed formats. Frequently, they first occur at an important moment. They may take place anytime that a student, immersed in some part of the reading process, collides with an inquiring teacher. These "quick encounters of the reading kind," yield important and pertinent information in a very short time.

~⁂~

Recording Information

Teachers use many methods of record keeping in the classroom. They create their own evaluation tools to fit their own curriculum needs. The record-keeping options are endless.

Anecdotal Notes

Anecdotal notes provide a wide variety of benefits for observing readers. Teachers record their observations of the reader's strengths, weaknesses, strategies used, growth, use of the reading process, attitude toward reading, comprehension or meaning-making ability, and any other important evidence of reading. Teachers usually write the anecdotal notes in phrases or "teacher shorthand." By recording

significant quotes, teachers capture the student's words verbatim. These expressive and meaningful quotes provide valuable information. Teachers share this information with parents or guardians during conferences. Dated anecdotes become a time line of the reader's progress.

Mailing labels provide a quick and easy way to manage anecdotal notes. Write the students' names on the labels. Teachers then attach the labels to a clipboard to use when those important "notable moments" occur. The labels peel off easily and adhere to a page in the child's assessment records.

Tonya

Ravi

Alyssa

Ben

Checklists

Checklists are versatile and adaptable and make a marvelous evaluation tool for recording any and all student actions. Checklists constructed for reading help guide the teacher's observations. If a teacher wants to look at certain aspects of the learners' reading process, those reading behaviors become part of the list. Teachers create checklists to meet the needs of the readers in the learning community. Checklists continuously grow and evolve as the readers progress through the year. The needs of the readers determine a variety of checklist styles.

NOTE: The samples here are reproduced full-size in the Appendix.

- **Individual Checklists—** Individual checklists record the growth of one individual student over a period of time. The checklist below allows the teacher to observe one student's use of the story elements during the study of one book. Teachers write the name of the student and the title of the book above a column of literature elements. Across the top of the grid are date boxes. This checklist is a practical tool to use during Literature Study Group sessions. By making a copy for each student, the teacher has access to each reader's record during dialogue sessions. As the students begin to share their logs and engage in dialogue, the teacher checks the appropriate literary elements as the student

interprets his or her thoughts. There is space at the bottom for detailed comments. This is another place for anecdotal notes. The checklist becomes a visual record of the literature elements most widely used by each reader. Observing individual patterns, allows the teacher to encourage students to gain deeper meaning by incorporating additional elements of the story.

- **Group Checklists—** Group checklists provide information about all students at once. Teachers use the group checklist to monitor certain observable actions in all of the students.
- **Other Types of Checklists—** Checklists are not always in the form of a grid. Some consist of check-off options of "yes" or "no" answers for certain reading behaviors. The quick "yes" or "no" used monthly shows growth over a long period of time. Another form of checklist uses words to assess the student's behavior. Words like *never*, *seldom*, *sometimes*, *usually* and *always*, provide broader options for assessment than the "yes" or "no" list.

Sample Checklist Questions

- *Do I rely on personal experiences to make meaning?*
- *Do I use pictures to help understand the story?*
- *Do I predict what will happen in the story?*
- *Do I use information I learned before to help me understand the story?*
- *Can I explain the mood of the story?*
- *Do I express how the story makes me feel?*

Rubrics

Rubrics are another form of recording a child's reading behavior and involvement with literature elements. They provide more information or explanation than a checklist, but unlike the teacher's written, anecdotal notes, rubrics present prescribed thoughts for the teacher to circle. Rubrics vary in size from three to six columns. Each column's descriptive phrase changes just enough to show a difference in the student's effort.

In the sample rubric on page 101, the student displays the action either *always, sometimes,* or *rarely.* The teacher observes the reader, and circles the descriptor that best fits the child's actions. Teachers create rubrics to match either particular situations or general ones that apply to many learning situations.

Sample Individual Checklist - Oral and Written Response to Literature

Name: *Joseph*

Book: *My Side of the Mountain*

Knowledge	4/3	4/5	4/7	4/11	4/13	4/17	4/19	4/21		
Setting	X									
Characters	X						X			
Narrator										
Details					X					
Comprehension										
Summarizes	X	X		X						
Sequence		X								
Mood							X			
Main Idea			X							
Figurative Language					X	X				
Application										
Draws Conclusions			X					X		
Illustrates			X	X						
States Examples								X		
Relates Personally		X	X		X	X		X		
Research										
Analysis										
Compare				X		X	X			
Contrast				X			X			
Debate						X				
Makes Generalizations						X		X		
Analyzes Problems										
Cause and Effect						X				
Synthesis										
Constructs New Meaning						X				
Predicts Outcome								X		
Formulates a Solution										
Creates New Ideas										
Write (story, poem, etc.)										
Evaluation										
Author's Purpose										
Critique										
Judges w/reasons										
Evaluates w/reasons										
Personal Opinion										

Session Comments:

Sample Group Checklist

Title/Author: _"Tuck Everlasting" by Natalie Babbit_

Student Names	Comes prepared for group	Has read assignment	Has written in Lit Log	Shares thoughts and ideas	
Natalie	X	X	X	X	
Robyn	X	X	X	X	
Jesse	X	X	X	X	
Jennifer	X	X		X	
Valerie		X	X		
Nathan		X		X	

Sample "Yes"/"No" Checklist

Name: *Levi*

Date: *April 21*

	Yes	No
Reads by choice	X	
Is prepared for lit. group	X	
Discusses with group	X	
Shares personal opinion		X

Sample Multiple Options Checklist

Name: _Levi_

Book: _"Tuck Everlasting"_

	Never	Seldom	Sometimes	Usually	Always
Analyzes characters			X		
Makes Predictions		X			
Connects situations				X	
Constructs new meaning		X			
Shares personal opinion	X				
Illustrates setting					X
Identifies cause and effect			X		
Compares/contrasts				X	
Reveals the author's purpose	X				
Debates issues		X			

Sample Literature Rubric

Name: *Jonathan*

Date: *April 21*

Reading Habits		
Reads independently by personal choice. **X**	Sometimes reads independently by personal choice.	Rarely reads independently by personal choice.
Reads from different genres without being prompted. **X**	Sometimes reads from different genres without being prompted.	Rarely reads from different genres without being prompted.
Talks to others about books.	Sometimes talks to others about books. **X**	Rarely talks to others about books.

Sample Self-Evaluation

Name: Fiona Campbell

Book: "Willy Wonka and the Chocolate Factory"

1. What did you learn during our literature study that you didn't realize before we discussed the book?

   I learned that "Veruca" means "wart" in Spanish, and she was nasty

   like a wart. The author gave her a name to symbolize her personality.

2. Tell about the best conversation that you remember in your lit group.

   Some people thought Willy Wonka was mean, and he kept the Oompa

   Loompas like slaves. I never thought of that before.

3. From which character did you learn an idea or a lesson? Explain.

   Charlie Bucket, because even though he was poor, he could be happy

   with what he had. He had love in his family.

4. Tell me how you feel about the author, how he/she writes, and why you think he/she wrote the book.

   I love Roald Dahl's books. His characters are funny and strange. I

   think he really understands being a kid, especially the bad parts.

5. Be a book critic. (Explain your own opinion of the book.)

   I enjoyed this book because it was fun to see the punishments that

   happened to all the bad children.

Analyzing Information

The most important part of evaluation is analyzing the gathered information and using it to develop a valuation. Patterns emerge from the accumulated assessment and form a picture of each student's ability to create meaning. From the emerging patterns, teachers identify strengths and weaknesses. This builds the foundation for each child's growth toward becoming a proficient reader. Teachers use the evaluation information to lead the readers into strategies that will increase their ability and desire to make meaning from the text.

Self-Evaluation

Self-evaluation invites the readers to examine their own progress. By critiquing their efforts, they begin to realize they are meaning makers. Students' self-evaluations open up an awareness of themselves as readers and thinkers. Reflection on past reading behaviors lead to greater understanding of future behaviors. Children reflect upon how they dealt with the story elements in a literature group, so that they can construct deeper meaning as they read on.

Children monitor their progress by recording their reflective thoughts. They write anecdotal notes in a reflective log or use the same kinds of checklists that teachers find helpful. These reflective checklists bring to mind those elements that may not have surfaced on their own.

Video-taping a literature session allows the students to see and hear themselves in action. Great discussions are born after students view the taped Literature Study Group. It is a wonderful tool for group evaluation. The members view their own actions in a group situation, so they can self-evaluate and group evaluate simultaneously. A written self-evaluation and group evaluation helps the individual group members reflect on insights gained from the group as a community of readers.

Reflection should take place daily. It becomes a natural part of the reading process.

Reflections

My answer to the child's question, "Wasn't lit group exciting today?" at the beginning of this chapter was a resounding, "Yes." Moreover I love the fact that the child was evaluating personal actions as well as the group's actions. Because children read, comprehend, reflect, self-evaluate and grow as meaning-makers, evaluation is ongoing and in a constant state of change. Evaluation is not the end of what a child can do. On the contrary, it is the beginning of what can be accomplished as children and literature unite. The child's thirst for enjoyment and knowledge is quenched by good literature.

— Penny

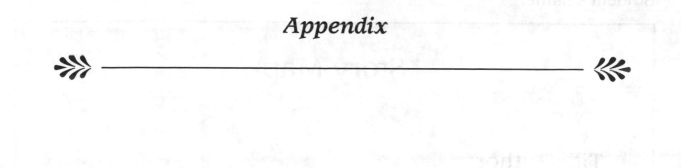

Blank
Reproducible
Forms

Student's name: _____

Story Map

Title/Author: _____

_____

Setting: _____

_____

Main Characters: _____

_____

Problem: _____

_____

_____

Events: _____

_____

_____

_____

Solutions: _____

_____

_____

Story Theme: _____

_____

_____

Story Grid

Title/ Author: _____

_____

1.	2.	3.	4.
5.	6.	7.	8.
9.	10.	11.	12.
13.	14.	15.	16.

Student's name: _____

Plot Chart
(Cause & Effect)

Title/Author: _____

_____

Event Happened	Event Caused	Resulting Effect

Student's name: _____

Character Map

Title/Author: _____

_____

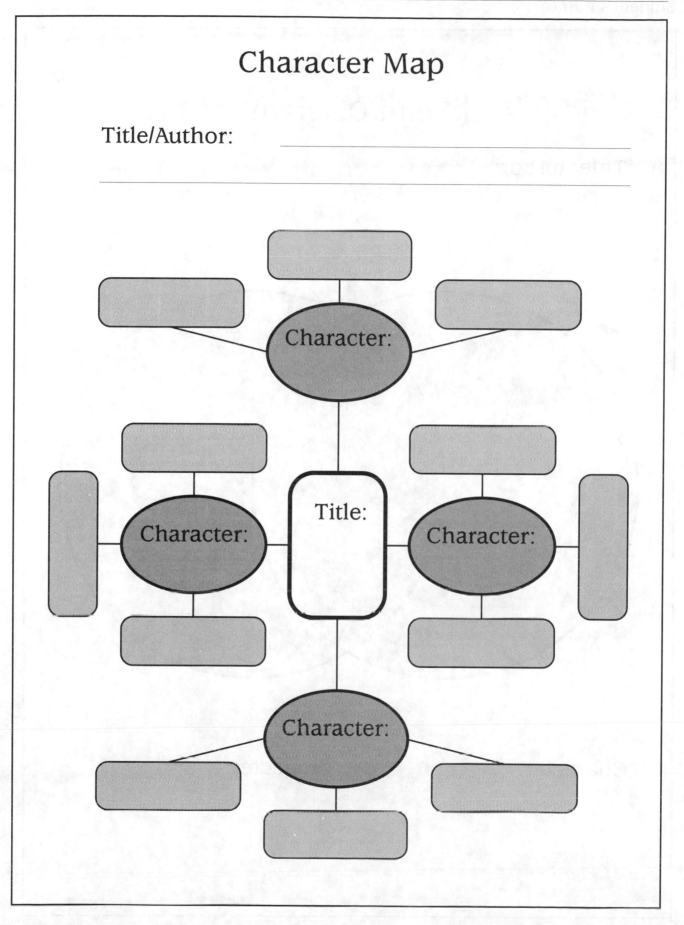

Student's name: _____

Venn Diagram

Title/Author: _____

_____

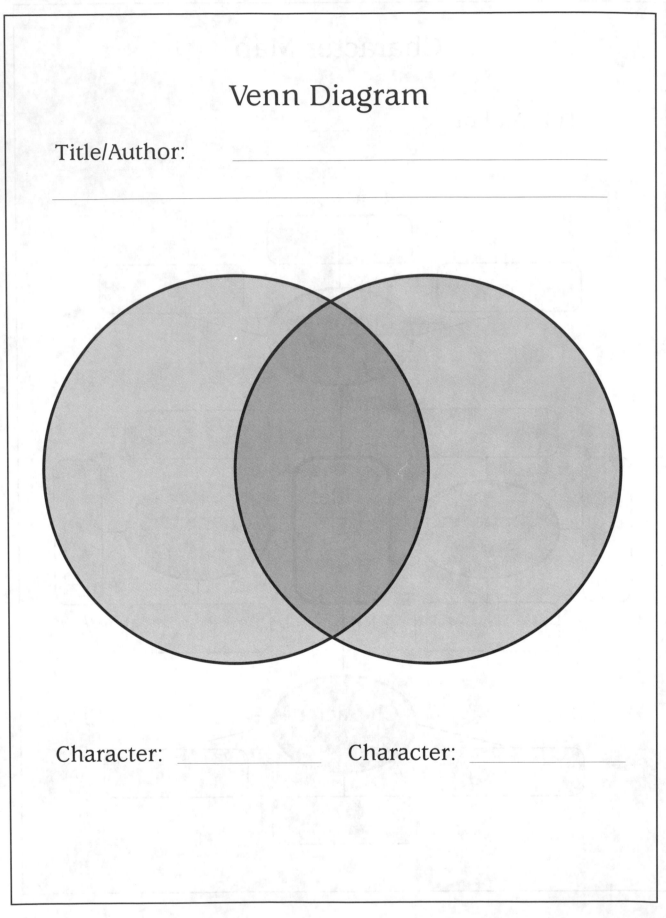

Character: _____   Character: _____

Student's name: _____

Prediction Chart #1

Title/Author: _____

_____

Clues from the Text	Your Interpretation	Your Prediction

Student's name: _____

Prediction Chart #2

Title/Author: _____

_____

Prediction Before Reading	Actual Happening

Individual Checklist - Oral and Written Response to Literature

Name:

Book:

Knowledge

Setting										
Characters										
Narrator										
Details										

Comprehension

Summarizes										
Sequence										
Mood										
Main Idea										
Figurative Language										

Application

Draws Conclusions										
Illustrates										
States Examples										
Relates Personally										
Research										

Analysis

Compare										
Contrast										
Debate										
Makes Generalizations										
Analyzes Problems										
Cause and Effect										

Synthesis

Constructs New Meaning										
Predicts Outcome										
Formulates a Solution										
Creates New Ideas										
Write (story, poem, etc.)										

Evaluation

Author's Purpose										
Critique										
Judges w/reasons										
Evaluates w/reasons										
Personal Opinion										

Session Comments:

Group Checklist

Title/Author: _____

_____

Student Names	Observable items					

"Yes"/"No" Checklist

Name: _____

Date: _____

	Yes	No

Multiple Options Checklist

Name: _____

Book: _____

	Never	Seldom	Sometimes	Usually	Always

Literature Rubric

Name: _____

Date: _____

Reading Habits		

Sample Self-Evaluation

Name: _____

Book: _____

1. What did you learn during our literature study that you didn't realize before we discussed the book?

_____

_____

2. Tell about the best conversation that you remember in your lit group.

_____

_____

3. From which character did you learn an idea or a lesson? Explain.

_____

_____

4. Tell me how you feel about the author, how he/she writes, and why you think he/she wrote the book.

_____

_____

5. Be a book critic. (Explain your own opinion of the book.)

_____

_____

Notes

Notes